W9-BKS-102

D. H. LAWRENCE
AND HUMAN EXISTENCE

D. H. LAWRENCE
and Human Existence

MARTIN JARRETT-KERR
of the Community of the Resurrection

FOREWORD BY
T. S. ELIOT

Chip's Bookshop
Booksellers & Publishers
New York

Standard Book Number 0-912378-03-4.

First published 1951
Second Edition SCM Press Ltd 1961
Reprinted, 1971, by Chip's Bookshop
with permission of
SCM Press Ltd.

Printed in the United States of America

CONTENTS

ACKNOWLEDGEMENT

THE author and publishers are grateful for permission to quote from the works of D. H. Lawrence, granted to this edition by Messrs Laurence Pollinger Ltd on behalf of the copyright holders.

FOREWORD

MY reason for contributing a preface to this book is that I think this is a serious piece of criticism of Lawrence, of a kind for which the time is now due. We have had a number of books about Lawrence by people who knew him; we need books about him by critics who know him only through his works. To have been associated with Lawrence was, evidently, for those who were attracted, or alternately attracted and repelled, by that dominating, cross-grained and extreme personality, a very important part of their lives, an experience which had to be recorded in print. But perhaps one of the reasons why Lawrence's books are now less read by young people than they were twenty or thirty years ago, is that the books about him give the impression that he is a man to read about, rather than an author to read: a Johnson surrounded by a shoal of Boswells, some of them less tender towards the great man than was Johnson's biographer.

This is not the only reason why Lawrence's work needs to be examined from a new perspective. He was an impatient and impulsive man (or so I imagine him to have been; for, like the author of this book, I never knew him). He was a man of fitful and profound insights, rather than of ratiocinative powers; and therefore he was an impatient man: he expressed some of his insights in the form least likely to make them acceptable to most of his contemporaries, and sometimes in a form which almost wilfully encouraged misunderstanding. If the foolish or the ill-disposed chose to regard him as a blasphemer, a ' fascist ', or a pornographer, Lawrence would not put himself out to persuade them. Wrong he often was (I think) from ignorance, prejudice, or drawing the wrong conclusions in his conscious mind from the insights which came to him from below consciousness: and it will take time to dissociate the superficial error from the fundamental truth. To me, also, he seems often to write very badly; but to be a writer who had to write often badly in order to write sometimes well. As for his religious attitude (of the development of which the author of this book has something to say) we can now begin to see better how much was ignorance, rather than hostility; for Lawrence was an ignorant man in the sense that he was unaware of how much he did not know. His strictures upon Christianity (and indeed upon Buddhism) are often ill-informed; at other times they go straight to the heart of the matter; and no Christian ought to feel sure that he is religious-minded enough, to ignore the criticism of a man who, without being a Christian, was primarily and always religious.

T. S. ELIOT

1951

INTRODUCTION

THIS book was first published in 1951, but it has been out of print for five or six years. It was written at a time when Lawrence's works were practically in eclipse. Indeed, in his Foreword which he kindly wrote for the book, Mr T. S. Eliot said that 'after being misunderstood, he (Lawrence) is in danger of being ignored.' That sentence is hardly necessary today—and has, indeed, been omitted from Mr Eliot's Foreword, which is of sufficient historic interest to be reprinted here.

In preparing this book for its second edition, I have thought it unnecessary to make any major alterations. A few corrections of fact, and a re-phrasing of one short paragraph, have seemed to me all that was required. In other words, my general assessment of Lawrence's greatness, and of his place in the kingdom of letters, remains precisely what it was ten years ago.

Nevertheless, much has happened during that ten years, upon some of which it is impossible not to make some comment. It is convenient to begin with the Preface to the first edition of this book, since some of what has happened since then was faintly foreseen then. Here is the relevant section of that 1951 Preface.

PREFACE OF 1951

Lawrence was once talking to Maurice Magnus:

> 'And if I think myself superior to the peasant, it is only that I feel myself like the growing tip . . . of the tree, and him like a piece of the hard, fixed tissue of the branch or trunk. We're part of the same tree: and it's exactly the same sap,' said I.
>
> 'Why, exactly! Exactly!' cried Magnus. 'Of course! The Church would teach the same doctrine. We are all one in Christ—but between our souls and our duties there are great differences.'

And Lawrence comments:

> It is terrible to be agreed with, especially by a man like Magnus. All that one says, and means, turns to nothing.[1]

[1] M. Magnus, *Memoirs of the Foreign Legion*, Secker, 1924, p. 40.

It is because Lawrence has been agreed with by the wrong people and for the wrong reasons that this book has been written. The adding of yet another to the multitudinous studies of Lawrence requires the sternest justification. Yet perhaps it is easier now, twenty years or so after his death, to see what in him is of lasting value. Certainly, few of the hasty books written then are of much critical worth; and now that his more enthusiastic camp-followers have disappeared the danger is more that he will be classed as *démodé* and neglected because of his obvious blemishes.

But there is a further reason for this book which ought to be presented frankly at the outset: that there does not seem yet to be any full-length study of Lawrence which approaches him specifically from the Christian point of view. Lest this at once suggest some form of Inquisitorial literary criticism, it must hastily be added that the primary object of approaching him from that position is that, in view of the abuse that has been hurled at him by so many Christians, it seemed that some amends from that quarter were overdue. Indeed, it is one of the themes of this book that Lawrence can teach Christians lessons they should have known but have forgotten. And when criticisms of him are here made they are made from out of a world-view which is relevant to art in a way that Lawrence's own world-view was relevant to his art. That is to say, this book agrees with Lawrence that there is no such thing as pure literary criticism abstracted from all moral and metaphysical judgements; in technical terms, that literary criticism must be not only aesthetic but also ' axiological ' and ' ontological '.

The manipulation of this kind of literary criticism will always be a delicate business; and not least upon an artist whose world-view is so compounded with his art as is that of Lawrence. Concretely, the danger is that, for instance, the opinions of characters in the novels are taken directly to be those of their creator. Sometimes in Lawrence's novels it just seems to be so; but then, when it is so there can always be detected a *literary* weakness in that very spot. In this book the attempt is made—with what success it is for others to judge—to do the detection.

One further warning. The first draft of this study was completed in 1948, when the neglect of Lawrence was perhaps at its deepest. Since then there has been something of a revival. Yet not enough, maybe, to render this book redundant. In detail, though the book claims no originality of research, there does not seem to be elsewhere any account of Lawrence which discusses the changes from the first to the final (third) drafts of *Lady Chatterley's Lover*: nor any which touches on Lawrence's relation to the much-publicized 'existentialist' movement of our time; nor which deals with the influence upon Lawrence of the 'pansexualism' of V. V. Rozanov. The treating of these was a further incentive to this book's composition.

D. H. LAWRENCE LITERATURE

So ran my Preface of 1951. Since then the Lawrence industry has been in fairly full employment. One or two further memoirs have appeared by people who knew him (however slightly) and there has been a number of critical studies in England and America. Of these, the most important is, of course, Dr F. R. Leavis' *D. H. Lawrence, Novelist* (Chatto, 1957), which gathers together his articles in *Scrutiny*, written over the years, and completes his early monograph—*D. H. Lawrence* (Minority Press, 1930)—by providing a full-scale treatment of the major novels and tales. It will be fairly clear from the text of my book that I am in closer agreement with Dr Leavis' than with Mr Eliot's judgment on Lawrence—which does not lessen, indeed rather the contrary, my gratitude to Mr Eliot for finding time, amid the pressure of other work, to read the manuscript and give encouragement to an unknown author who ventured to take issue with him on some points. Dr Leavis, in a well-known article, assailed Mr Eliot for his Foreword; but he perhaps underestimated the extent of the change in Mr Eliot's views which this Foreword marked—a change which is also exhibited by his refusal to reissue *After Strange Gods*.

There have also been biographies of Lawrence and new editions of many of his works, including some of his letters. One of the strangest events was the reissue, in 1954, of John Middleton Murry's *Son of Woman*, with a new Introduction. This extraordinary book was first published in 1931 and is generally regarded by critics as among the worst books that that brilliant, uneven, intuitive writer ever produced. Mr Aldous Huxley described it as an 'essay in destructive hagiography', and, besides containing some very eccentric judgements on Lawrence's work (Murry dismisses *Women in Love* and *St Mawr*, but exalts *Aaron's Rod* to the supreme position among the novels), the book reveals much more about Murry than it does about Lawrence. Here are some characteristic passages from *Son of Woman* (1954 ed.):

> 'This man (Lawrence), we feel, has no business with sex at all. He is born to be a saint; then let him be one, and become a eunuch for the sake of the Kingdom of Heaven. For him, we prophesy, sex must be one long laceration, one long tortured striving for the unattainable . . . (p. 36).
>
> The Reader will be aghast at the intensity of loathing for woman in the sex relation which Lawrence felt and uttered at the end of his life (p. 46).
>
> Lawrence was incapable of loving a woman (p. 96).
>
> (Annable, in the *White Peacock*, had said 'Be a good animal, true to your animal instinct'). No mistake is possible. Annable's creed is the same as Mellors' creed (sc., in *Lady Chatterley*); it is the creed which Lawrence eventually came to proclaim openly (p. 46).

It was hardly to be expected that Murry, who had (despite his enormous admiration for Lawrence) quarrelled with him, and also fallen in love with Frieda (she became for a brief while his mistress after Lawrence's death) [2], could only two or three years later have written an objective, impartial book on Lawrence. Yet in his Introduction to the 1954 reissue Murry, though he admits that his book was one-sided and says that if he were rewriting it he would now write it differently, does not in fact take back any of his curious judgements on Lawrence. He does say that Lawrence

> was the living embodiment of yet another theory which is part of the intellectual climate of today: the philosophy of existentialism. We need not look abroad for instruction into the reality of existential thinking. Lawrence, once more, is the thing itself. [3]

[2] 'If I had gone with Lawrence and Frieda (to Mexico), Frieda would have become my woman', wrote Murry in his Journal. F. A. Lea, *John Middleton Murry*, Methuen, 1959, p. 119.

[3] Murry, *Son of Woman*, p. xiv.

And this tallies with what I have tried to say in my study. But by reprinting the book as it stood, without any substantial recantation in the Introduction, Murry perpetuated his partial, and often distorted, interpretation of Lawrence. And what makes it even more strange: only two years later he is writing of Lawrence in a much more appreciative, level-headed vein, in an essay which appeared in *Love, Freedom and Society* (1957). The trend of it can be summarized by quoting from his Journal of the time.

> The simple mystery of life—the infinite mystery of it. Lawrence enlarged our awareness of it: brought together our bodies and our souls. We shall never be the same as we were before him. We struggle with him and, though he does not prevail, his virtue passes into us. We have been quickened.[4]

Witter Bynner's reminiscences, *Journey with Genius* (1951), came out too late for me to be able to use it in my book; but, though Murry seems to have found it informative about the later Lawrence, there is nothing in it that would make me wish to alter my own picture. Of Mr Richard Aldington's biography I had this to say in the Preface to my book:

> *Portrait of a Genius, But* . . . (19) appeared after the completion of the present book. But as it has been described as the definitive study, a word must be said about it. As a factual account it is valuable;[5] but it will be clear to the reader that its interpretation of Lawrence's thought differs considerably from that put forward in the following pages. Indeed in two instances there is here an almost direct contravention of Mr Aldington's views.
>
> In the first chapter below will be found a very radical qualification of the opinion expressed in Mr Aldington's words that 'among his contemporaries Lawrence chiefly admired insignificant writers, and had poor literary judgement,' (p. 182). And in another place Mr Aldington says that Lawrence indignantly rejected 'the Christian notion that sex is merely a hindrance to salvation' (p. 106). The whole of the present book may be considered a disputing of that statement as a description of Christian belief. It is only fair to note that Mr Aldington in his biography explicitly declares that he has tried to avoid literary criticism. What is questionable is whether anyone can write a book on Lawrence and evade the responsibility of literary criticism.

[4] Quoted in F. A. Lea, *op. cit.*, p. 348.
[5] Less so now, in 1961, since the more scholarly lives have appeared.

Mr Graham Hough's *The Dark Sun* (1957) fails to break new ground, and repeats the same popular misinterpretation of Christianity. He speaks of 'The Christian depreciation of sexuality', and adds in a footnote:

> I take it for granted that Christianity does depreciate sexuality, or at most make *(sic)* reluctant concessions to it; and that Lawrence was right in believing this, wherever else he was wrong; and that the Chestertonian (and post-Chestertonian) trick of representing Christianity as a robustly Rabelasian sort of faith is a vulgar propagandist perversion (p. 246).

But Mr Hough's account of *The Man Who Died* seems to me the one excellent thing in an otherwise undistinguished book; and as I am conscious that in my own book the place given to that moving and important long story of Lawrence's is quite inadequate, I gladly refer to Mr Hough's discussion of it. Some Christians have found the story shocking or blasphemous. But of course, 'The Man' is merely a Jewish prophet and although he clearly represents Lawrence's conception of Jesus of Nazareth he is careful never to give him a name. And I think Mr Hough is right when he says that it is not merely

> the story of a particular man at a particular time, but (as) an allegory of the course of Christian civilization. The death of the prophet is also a symbol of the death of the Christian dispensation. Christian civilization is dying after two thousand years. But the story of man is a continuity, and no culture ever really dies: it comes to life again, to a new life...
>
> The second part of the story is a foreshadowing of the new dispensation that is to come... The fleshly tenderness that is to replace Christian love in the new order can never be the pristine, unembarrassed pagan delectation... Christianity may be brought into touch again with the old nature-mysteries of death and re-birth, as it is in this tale; but they will be changed in the process (p. 252).

This is well put, and those who still believe in the survival of something called 'Christendom' would do well to heed what Lawrence is saying here.

One of the pleasant results of writing a book is the friends it can sometimes make for the writer. I consider myself fortunate in having made through my book the brief acquaintance, before he died in 1955, of Mr S. S. Koteliansky, who of course knew Lawrence intimately. He corrected my conjecture (p. 112

below) that he had spoken to Lawrence about Rozanov. But he was able to confirm, from first hand, some of the judgements in my book. In particular he said that 'Yes, Lawrence was a deeply, deeply religious man. Unlike that utterly irreligious woman, his wife.'

But the friendship I chiefly value, arising from the book, is with Mr Harry T. Moore, the great Lawrence scholar. His biography, *The Intelligent Heart* (first published in the USA in 1955, and republished in a new and revised edition by Penguin Books in 1960) is the most thorough, balanced, and wisely appreciative popular biography that we are ever likely to have. He has also (with Frederick J. Hoffman) produced a useful book of excerpts from standard critical studies of Lawrence (*The Achievement of D. H. Lawrence*, University of Oklahoma Press, 1953); a volume of recent essays (*A D. H. Lawrence Miscellany*, Southern Illinois University Press and Heinemann); and, above all, the two-volume new edition of Lawrence's *Letters*, which, incorporating as it does many recent finds, is likely to be the definitive edition when it comes (late 1961). Mr Moore has been helpful as well as encouraging, and combines exactitude and persistence in tracking down biographical details with a fine perception of values.

No doubt there are many books that I have missed. But I do not think that any new discoveries are likely to alter the picture we now have of the man and his work.

THE LADY CHATTERLEY TRIAL

There is one event, since this book first appeared, which can not be ignored, however disproportionate the attention paid to it may seem in retrospect to have been: the 'Trial of Lady Chatterley'. For a week during the actual trial of Messrs Penguin Books Ltd, for publishing 'an obscene book, *viz. Lady Chatterley's Lover*', conducted at the Old Bailey, and for many weeks after it, the publicity in the newspapers, in correspondence columns, on the radio, in sermons and the rest, was unprecedented. This publicity was also of considerable sociological and theological significance, and it is as such that I propose to discuss it here.

My evaluation of the novel itself can be found in the following pages—which remain substantially as I wrote them more than ten years ago before any controversy was abroad. If I were writing about the novel today I should perhaps place it slightly higher than I did in 1951. I should, for instance, say more of the delicate beauty of much of the descriptive writing, and of the gentle tact of most (if not of quite all) the erotic passages. But I should still insist on the sad, shut-in quality of the book, on its final failure to convince the reader that here is a genuine way out from the underground of our dead culture into the open air of new discovery. And therefore I should assess its relation to the rest of Lawrence's work as in some ways roughly equivalent to the position of *Timon of Athens* in the corpus of Shakespeare's plays.

Nevertheless, Shakespeare without *Timon* is not Shakespeare. And this must be the sufficient reason for publishing *Lady Chatterley* openly in place of a clandestine circulation. The reasons given for continuing the ban on the novel were, of course, moral and social, not literary; but they all assumed that Lawrence's stature was simply not adequate to provide reasons for publication which would (as they have with the great classics of our literature) outweigh the reasons (of reticence, propriety, etc.) which might tell against publication. If such an assumption —of literary stature—is challenged, as in fact it was by some seventy competent literary and other ' experts ', there is nothing more to be said.

But the arguments employed by those wishing to retain the ban on the book (both during the trial and after) revealed two widespread convictions which show that Lawrence's work is still far from being completed.

First, they revealed an attitude to sex which, though perhaps less restrictive than it might have been thirty years ago, is still far short of the full, glad appreciation of divine-human creativity, of gratitude for the body, which should be the mark of a truly Christian theological view. Perhaps not many who supported the case for the Prosecution would have subscribed to the view of one correspondent, who wrote to the *Times* of 10 November in the following terms:

> The great majority of us do feel a very decided reticence about copulation, which has its cause, I expect, in the crudity and indignity of the act. Nature really might have thought of something else!

But there was certainly in most of them an assumption that 'reverence' for the sexual relation and reticence about it are inseparable if not synonymous; and a further, sometimes clearly stated, assumption that the relation between Connie and Mellors—and therefore the relation recommended by Lawrence—was 'purely animal'. Unfortunately John Middleton Murry (in *Son of Woman*) gave strong support to this proposition. But it simply is not true. The novel is now obtainable by all, and, read in the context of all Lawrence's writings, should be in itself sufficient refutation to any careful and sympathetic reader.

It is distressing that this 'Prosecution' view should in many cases have been based on 'Christian moral principles'. We only have to read the alterations made in the language of the Authorized Version of the Bible of 1611 by the Revisers of 1884 to see how considerably conventions in terminology or vocabulary can change. (At least one 'four-letter word' was removed in 1884. It reminds one that in the expurgated edition of *Lady Chatterley* among other words deleted was the good old Biblical, four-letter 'womb'.) That the standards of nineteenth century, or even of Edwardian, prudery should be taken as *Christian* standards seems to me not merely silly but theologically disastrous. This does not mean that I think Lawrence was right in believing that he could effect a revolution in our use of, or attitude towards, words which (though they might be decently and even reverently used by an imaginary gamekeeper) are normally considered vulgar if not obscene. I think Lawrence was being (to use an adjective which he would have regarded as a terrible insult) idealistic, or at least unrealistic in thinking he could. But this is not to deny the perfect seriousness of his attempt; and I am sure that one of the reasons which decided the jury in the Trial to return a verdict of Not Guilty was that in fact the growing familiarity with the language, in the context of Lawrence's matchless prose, did do something to effect in them the very revolution Lawrence hoped for. The significance of this (if the conjecture is true) has perhaps been as yet insufficiently appreciated; for, unless indeed twelve men and women of the jury were for ever 'corrupted and depraved' during the first week of November 1960, it is hard to see how the Crown case could be proved.

But the other conviction that evidently lay behind most of the arguments for the Prosecution is in the long run a still more disastrous one. It is, briefly, that literature exists to promote moral behaviour. This is certainly the negative conclusion to be drawn from such a passage as the famous *Times* Leader of 3 November:

> It is hard to make the major premise of the book other than that Constance Chatterley was behaving naturally in being unchaste both before and throughout marriage and was justified in lying with one man after another until she found one to her satisfaction.

The same conclusion is implied in the more directly denunciatory tones of certain clerical pronouncements, such as:

> Many of us believe that it (the novel) will be a powerful instrument of the Devil in greatly increasing the already immense quantity of evil literature ... God meant sex to be clean—Humanity has got the whole thing out of focus (Archdeacon T. Dilworth-Harrison).

Or, from a prominent Church weekly:

> The relationship between Lady Chatterley and her lover in this novel is not lawful marriage. It is adultery, and nothing but adultery ... Nothing can invalidate the Seventh Commandment. For guidance in morals the Church must continue to look, not to such as Lawrence, but to the Living God.
>
> *Church Times,* Leader, 11 November 1960.

And the argument was driven home a week later, insisting on

> ... the simple issues involved. They are not issues of abstruse intellectual categories and concepts, but of good and evil, right and wrong ... What is needed in an age of sexual licence is a positive restatement of old and simple distinctions, between purity and lust, between sacraments and sins, between marriage and adultery, between the Christian worship of God and the pagan worship of sex. There is nothing in the least 'intelligent' in calling evil good, and good evil.

There is in all this, to begin with, simply a failure of attention: those who can write like this have not really *read* Lawrence. I don't mean, have not passed their eyes over his text (though many who voiced views similar to these above admitted that they had not even done that), but have not read him with the kind of imaginative sympathy and sensitiveness required for genuine understanding of great literature. Even at the level here assumed, *viz.* of dealing not with imaginative literature but with 'moral theology', is there to be no discrimination between different types of sexual 'misconduct'? Is the one blanket word 'adultery' to be used for (for instance) some of Connie's promiscuous and empty love-affairs, the adultery *recommended by her own husband* with someone of her own class to give her a child, and her liaison with Mellors?

Secondly, those who express such views seem not to be living in our world but in an imaginary world of 'Christendom'. The novelist, after all, is the artist who has to live closest to, and to express most directly, the phenomena of twentieth-century society: and that means, of a post-Christian society. Is he, even if he is a non-Christian (as Lawrence was), to lift himself out of this society and to create a fairy-story world in which the Ten Commandments are universally observed and the correct theological terminology everywhere employed? Or, to put it in another way, are Christians unable to make any distinctions between novels which depict adultery with a casual and cynical kind of irresponsibility (such as, to take a recent example, J. G. Cozzens' *By Love Possessed*) and those which deal with adulterous situations but in a way that shows compassion for the protagonists and awareness of tragedy?

And finally, have we got to accept the directly didactic view of art which these statements for the Prosecution imply? I do not, of course, wish to plead for aestheticism, for the doctrine of 'art for art's sake'; and indeed the problem of the relation of morals to literature is (like the similar problem of the relation of belief to literature, to which whole books, my own among them, have been devoted) both delicate and intricate. But two things can be said, briefly and vigorously. First, any work of imaginative literature which set out deliberately to influence conduct in an ethically correct direction would turn out to be simply a bad work of art (and if this is any comfort to the Prosecution, so would any work which set out deliberately to influence conduct in an ethically bad direction). And secondly, Christians who are not prepared to sit down and learn from great non-Christian artists—from Homer, Sophocles, Virgil, Ovid, Lucretius, Kalidisa, Goethe, Thomas Mann, W. B. Yeats, D. H. Lawrence, and the remaining cloud of witnesses—are cutting themselves off from some truth about the world. And if all truth comes ultimately from God, that means depriving themselves of some knowledge of God. Whatever criticisms the Christian theologian may have of Lawrence (and he cannot but have many) a true understanding of his positive contributions will enlarge the very concepts with which the theologian does his criticizing.

The judgment of Christians who spoke for the Prosecution shows that the misrepresentations of such as Mr Aldington and Mr Hough, given above, are understandable enough. In the words of my first Preface, amends from the Christian quarter are still overdue. Christians, it seems to me, owe a debt to Lawrence for insisting again and again that man is not without a body, and expresses himself as man not without his body. And what Lawrence says about sex is true even more widely. The Christian should know—though he often forgets—that sex involves three surrenders. First, there is the surrender of the self to the other (the man to the wife, the wife to the man). Then, and this is most easily evaded, there is the surrender of the mind, of the thinking, conscious self, to the instinctive self, in fact, to the body. And finally, there is the surrender of these two surrenders to God—to God who (so to speak) thought it all up, whose idea it was, who established the process. And this is true of more than just sex. For all human life at its highest and best involves: first, the personal relationship of love and fidelity; and then the co-operation with, the working along the lines of, the natural processes of the physical and social orders; and finally, the rendering of all this to God who can give the whole thing a purpose. Unless Christian preaching is a preaching to the whole of man, which includes the second stage, man's instinctual, bodily, and archetypal self, then it is partial and maimed. If, in all his work, Lawrence helped (in Murry's words) to ' bring together our bodies and souls ', then, no doubt unconsciously and almost in spite of himself, he did something of great importance in the Christian scheme of things. This book is a slight token of the gratitude that Christians should owe him.

January 1961 MARTIN JARRETT-KERR, C.R.

Post Script

In an essay ' The Myth of *The Plumed Serpent* ', published in *A D. H. Lawrence Miscellany,* ed. Harry T. Moore (Heinemann, 1961), Mr Jascha Kessler has produced one of the first rehabilitations—interesting, though not, I think, wholly convincing—of Lawrence's *The Plumed Serpent.* In the course of it Mr Kessler refers to my book and says ' Father Tiverton . . . is concerned in his study to interpret Lawrence as a kind of Existential Christian ' (p. 251). Since other critics have also taken my book in this way—Dr Leavis, for instance, has said that he views ' with the gravest distrust the prospect of his (Lawrence's) being adopted for expository appreciation as almost a Christian by writers whose religious complexion is congenial to Mr Eliot ' (*Scrutiny*, vol. xviii, p. 72)—I should like to make it clear, since I do not seem to have done so, that I do not want to claim Lawrence as any kind of a Christian; I have merely tried to establish certain parallels.

CHAPTER ONE

POET OR PRIEST?

I. SELF-CRITICISM

> 'Of course', said Gudrun easily, 'there is a quality of life in Birkin which is quite remarkable. There is an extraordinary rich spring of life in him, really amazing, the way he can give himself to things. But there are so many things in life that he simply doesn't know. Either he is not aware of their existence at all, or he dismisses them as merely negligible—things which are vital to the other person. In a way, he is not clever enough, he is too intense in spots.'
>
> 'Yes,' cried Ursula, 'too much of a preacher. He is really a priest.'
>
> 'Exactly! He can't hear what anybody else has to say—he simply cannot hear. His own voice is so loud.'
>
> 'Yes. He cries you down.' [1]

D. H. LAWRENCE has always presented a problem to the literary critic. Mr Aldous Huxley says categorically that 'Lawrence was always and unescapably an artist'.[2] Mr Middleton Murry, on the other hand, is emphatic that 'Lawrence was not, primarily, "an artist"; he knew it, he declared it, his books reveal it'.[3] And Mr Murry wrote *Son of Woman* largely in order to show that Lawrence's 'life was an allegory and his works are the comment on it'. This view must be rejected if only for the reason that long after the biographies and personal records have faded from memory the novels and poems will still be there for judgement. But the former view still has its difficulties: for there is so much of the pure 'prophet' in Lawrence—and in

[1] *Women in Love*, Secker, 1921, (cap. XIX).
[2] Aldous Huxley, Introduction to *The Letters of D. H. Lawrence*, Heinemann, 1932.
[3] J. Middleton Murry, *Reminiscences of D. H. Lawrence*, Secker, 1933, p. 167.

creasingly so as he grew older—that the critic approaching him from the point of view of pure 'literary criticism' is tempted, whatever his admiration, to endorse the usual (but, as we hope to show, superficial) verdict that Lawrence showed great promise in his early novels, but started to go off on a barren track with *The Rainbow*, and from then on ceases to be of value to 'literature' except in occasional purple passage or books of pure description. Mrs Carswell[4] only records a widespread opinion when she says that at one time she thought that the Lawrence of *The White Peacock* and *Sons and Lovers* might have developed into the Dickens of the Nottinghamshire coalfields. Some of the established writers and critics of the time saw in these two novels the marks of a new young writer of great power. And then (so runs the account) this coming novelist ceases to be interested in characters, starts entertaining strange ideas, and is overwhelmed by the sensuous rhythm of his own imagination. From now on we can cease to expect from him anything but exhortations, musings and vituperations, save for those moments when the sheer beauty of a scene seizes him by the beard as he strides along, and detains him till he has evoked it with his marvellous prose.

There are two facts, however, which make us pause before accepting this familiar judgement: one is Lawrence's self-awareness, and the other is his acutely critical intellect. Both these elements in Lawrence have been so largely ignored that we must spend some time in illustrating them.

Lawrence is perfectly aware of what he is doing, and aware of the criticisms that will be directed upon him. He could see that people would not understand the direction he is taking. At moments we find him hesitating ('Perhaps I am too self-important', he writes to Lady Cynthia Asquith in 1915;[5]) though in the novels, the work of mature consideration, he is always confident that he is on the right lines.

[4] C. Carswell, *Savage Pilgrimage,* Chatto and Windus, 1932.
[5] *Letters,* p. 259.

But even there he gives his critics a fair chance. We have quoted a good instance of this at the head of this section: if for Gudrun we read Katherine Mansfield, for Ursula Frieda, and for Birkin Lawrence, we see that he has given ample scope to Counsel for the Prosecution. The famous scene from the same novel, *Women in Love,*[6] in the Pompadour Café is another instance. Gudrun and Gerald overhear some 'arty' young men and women discussing and laughing about a letter one of them has received from Birkin. They are all a bit drunk, and one of them, Halliday, reads out the letter mockingly as if preaching a sermon. Gudrun, furious at the insult to Birkin, slips up to them and asks to see the letter. They give it to her unsuspecting, and she strides out of the Café with it before they can stop her. Now the interesting thing about this is that, according to Mr Murry,[7] this scene actually took place. Some young men (and it is known that Philip Heseltine—'Peter Warlock'—understood Halliday to refer to himself) were overheard by Katherine Mansfield joking about Lawrence's volume of poetry, *Amores,* and she did what Gudrun did. But in the novel Lawrence loads the dice against himself even more heavily by turning the book of poems into a letter from Birkin; and, moreover, a letter which reads like an exaggerated version of Lawrence's own mystical philosophy of the time. 'There is a phase in every race when the desire for destruction overcomes every other desire . . . It is a desire for the reduction-process in oneself, a reducing back to the origin, a return along the Flux of Corruption, to the original rudimentary conditions of being. . . . Surely there will come an end in us to this desire—for the constant going apart—this passion for putting asunder—everything—ourselves . . . reducing the two great elements of male and female from their highly complex unity—reducing the old ideas, going back to the savages for our

[6] *Women in Love,* Secker, 1921, (cap. XVII), as above [1].
[7] J. Middleton Murry, *Reminiscences of D. H. Lawrence,* 1933, p. 95, as above [3].

sensations—always seeking to *lose* ourselves in some ultimate black sensation, mindless and infinite—burning only with destructive fires, raging on with the hope of being burnt out utterly...' This is the letter which is read, punctuated with hiccups, and interspersed with giggling comments, in the tone of a clergyman reading the lessons. Lawrence has here produced a perfect self-parody; and a writer who can do that, without losing control of the novel, knows what he is doing.

The point is worth labouring, for Lawrence is so often represented as the obstinate, temperamental, predative emotionalist; 'the brilliant undisciplined, self-indulgent, anarchistic authoritarian, with all his sophisticated primitivism, emotional naïveté, and utter impracticality' is how, for instance, Mr Eric Bentley describes him.[8] Yet what about passages like this: 'If ever I have abused you', he writes to a correspondent, 'I am very sorry and ashamed. But I don't think I have: though Heaven knows what one says.... We have *often* laughed at you, because you are one of those special figures one can laugh at; just as I am, only I'm ten times more ridiculous. But I'm sure we've laughed kindly and affectionately....'[9] Or: 'The Holy Ghost bids us never to be deadly in our earnestness, always to laugh in time, at ourselves and everything. Particularly at our sublimities.'[10] Frieda once observed to Mabel Dodge Luhan that Lawrence 'has to get it all from me. Unless I am there he feels nothing. Nothing. And he gets his books from me.... Nobody knows that. Why, I have done pages of his books for him. In *Sons and Lovers* I actually wrote pages into it.'[11] But Lawrence himself was well aware of this dependence. In *Aaron's Rod* we find:

> 'My hand doesn't need holding,' snapped Lilly.
> 'Doesn't it.' (said Tanny, his wife) 'More than most

[8] Eric Bentley, *Cult of the Superman,* Hale, 1947, p. 230.
[9] *Letters,* Heinemann, 1932, p. 321.
[10] D. H. Lawrence: *Studies in Classical American Literature,* Secker, 1924, p. 76.
[11] M. D. Luhan, *Lorenzo in Taos,* Secker, 1933, p. 58.

men's! But you're so beastly ungrateful and mannish. Because I hold you safe enough all the time, you like to pretend you're doing it all yourself.'[12]

Lilly, of course, is Lawrence, and Tanny is Frieda. And in *Kangaroo,* where Somers is Lawrence and Harriet is Frieda, we find a surprisingly intimate self-revelatory chapter, 'At Sea in Marriage', describing the ebb and flow in their relationship.

> 'He had nothing but her, [muses Harriet] absolutely. And that was why, presumably, he wanted to establish this ascendency over her, assume this arrogance.... She could *not* stand these world-saviours. And she, she must be safely there, as a nest for him, when he came home with his feathers pecked. That was it. So that he could imagine himself absolutely and arrogantly It, he would turn her into a nest, and sit on her and overlook her, like the one and only phoenix in the desert of the world, gurgling hymns of salvation. Poor Harriet! No wonder she resented it! Such a man, such a man to be tied to and tortured by!'[13]

So, too, Lawrence is perfectly aware of the criticisms of his cult of mindlessness, and of globe-trotting. 'Magic of the animal world!' roared Kangaroo to Somers, in the same novel. 'What does that nonsense mean? Are you traitor to your own human intelligence?'[14] And Jaz later pulls Somers' leg: 'Seems to me you just go round the world looking for things you're not going to give in to.'[15]

This self-criticism applies to his writing also. He did not easily accept the criticism of others, but his pertinacity in perfecting his own craft is surprising. He never revised, he rewrote, and sometimes rewrote his whole novels, right through, two and even three times over. Writing to Edward Garnett about the final draft of *Women in Love,* he describes the travail that gave birth to it. 'In the *Sisters* was the germ of this novel: woman becoming individual, self-

[12] *Aaron's Rod,* Secker, 1923, (cap. VIII, p. 87).
[13] *Kangaroo,* Secker, 1924, pp. 195-6.
[14] *ibid.,* p. 231.
[15] *ibid.,* p. 390.

responsible, taking her own initiative. But the first *Sisters* was flippant and often vulgar and jeering. I had to get out of that attitude, and make my subject really worthy . . . I have very often the vulgarity and disagreeableness of the common people, as you say Cockney, and I may be a Frenchman. But primarily I am a passionately religious man. . . . And my Cockneyism and commonness are only when the deep feeling doesn't find its way out, and a sort of jeer comes instead, and sentimentality, and purplism. But you should see the religious, earnest, suffering man in me first, and then the flippant or common things after. Mrs Garnett says I have no true nobility—with all my cleverness and charm. But that is not true. It is there, in spite of all the littlenesses and commonnesses.' [16] If the sign of the submerging of poetry by preaching is the absence of self-criticism, then we cannot, I think, accuse Lawrence of this.

II. THE LITERARY CRITIC

The second fact which makes us pause before accepting the usual verdict on Lawrence is his acutely critical intellect, especially as seen in his literary criticism. In an article written in 1925, 'Accumulated Mail', [17] he deals trenchantly with various objections against his writing, and especially that 'Lawrence is an artist, but his intellect is not up to his art'. He replies: 'You might as well say: Mr Lawrence rides a horse but he doesn't wear his stirrups round his neck. And the accusation is just. Because he hopes to heaven he is riding a horse that is alive of itself, not a wooden hobbyhorse suitable for the nursery. And he does his best to keep his feet in the stirrups, and to leave his intellect under his hat. . . . No, my dears! I guess, as an instrument, my intellect is as good as yours. But instead of

[16] *Letters,* p. 190.
[17] *Phoenix,* Heinemann, 1936, p. 805.

sitting on my own wheelbarrow (the intellect is a sort of wheelbarrow about the place) and whipping it ecstatically over the head, I just wheel out what dump I've got, and forget the old barrow again, till next time.' Mr T. S. Eliot, whose strictures are fairer than most, has charged Lawrence with 'lack of intellectual and social training';[18] and expanded this by saying that 'Lawrence, even had he acquired a great deal more knowledge and information than he ever came to possess, would always have remained uneducated. By being "educated" I mean having such an apprehension of the contours of the map of what has been written in the past, as to see instinctively where everything belongs and approximately where anything new is likely to belong; it means, furthermore, being able to allow for all the books one has not read and the things one does not understand—it means some understanding of one's own ignorance.'[19] Dr Leavis has replied to this accusation in an article on 'The Wild, Untutored Phoenix',[20] and here I find myself in agreement with Dr Leavis. It is true that Lawrence never did a University course (his time at Nottingham was only two years, doing a course in Education). And he does say of himself that 'in education, I'm merely scrappy'.[21] But from the *Memoir*[22] by his old friend 'E. T.' (Miriam of *Sons and Lovers*) we can get an idea of the width of his early reading. We know that he had a flair for picking up languages (even if with an atrocious accent): French, German, Spanish, Italian, and even sufficient Sicilian to translate the difficult dialect works of Verga. On the subject of translation he observes pertinently of Jowett's *Plato:* 'The gulf between Prof. Jowett's mentality and Plato's mentality is almost impassible. . . . Plato divorced from his pagan background is only another Victorian statue in toga—

[18] T. S. Eliot, *After Strange Gods,* Faber, 1933, p. 59.
[19] Essay in *Revelation,* edited by Baillie and Martin, Faber, 1937.
[20] *Scrutiny,* vol. VI, no. 3, December, 1937; *cf.* vol. XVI, no. 3, September, 1949.
[21] Knud Merrild, *A Poet and Two Painters,* Secker, 1938, p. 206.
[22] 'E. T.', *D. H. Lawrence, A Memoir,* Cape, 1935.

or a chlamys '[23]—which reminds us of certain remarks by Mr Eliot himself on Prof. Gilbert Murray's translation of Euripides. Above all, from the *Letters* and the scattered reviews collected in *Phoenix,* we get the impression of a surprising width of culture. True, his fierce personal prejudices sometimes spoil his judgements—*e.g.*, of Pope, Tolstoy, Dostoievsky, Joyce, and Eliot himself. And yet there are surprises constantly awaiting us: witness his admiration for Manzoni's *I Promessi Sposi,* read by hardly anyone else, and a work of orthodox Catholic *pietas* which one might not have thought to Lawrence's taste.[24] And on direct criticism he is frequently excellent. Every essay in the *Studies in Classical American Literature* (1924) has something acute, and the account of Poe and of Melville's *Moby Dick* are of permanent critical value—and that in a field which was at the time almost untouched. The essay on John Galsworthy (1928) is cruel but to my mind entirely right.[25] It is easy to dismiss his hostility as mere revenge for Galsworthy's failure to give him adequate encouragement as a struggling young writer; but he is in fact generous to Galsworthy's positive achievements, while putting his finger exactly on the weak spots. 'Galsworthy had not quite enough of the superb courage of his satire. He faltered, and gave in to the Forsytes . . .'; and 'it is when he comes to sex that Galsworthy collapses finally. He becomes nastily sentimental. He wants to make sex important, and he only makes it repulsive. . . . The sexual level is extraordinarily low, like dogs.' Compare, too, his reference to Galsworthy's *Strife,* in the Preface to his own play—a poor play—*Touch and Go* (1919): he argues that a miners' strike should provide a good theme for modern drama, but says that 'As yet no one tackles this situation. . . . Mr Galsworthy had a peep and sank down towards bathos '.[26]

[23] *Apocalypse,* Orioli, Florence, 1931, (cap. IX, p. 131).
[24] *Phoenix,* Introduction to Verga, *Mastro-don Gesualdo,* pp. 223ff.
[25] *Phoenix,* pp. 542-6.
[26] *Touch and Go,* Secker, 1919.

He has some fine comic reviewing of modern poetry in his account of 'A Second Contemporary Verse Anthology' (1923).[27] And few writers have 'placed' H. G. Wells better than Lawrence (who had once admired his novels) in a review in 1926 called 'The World of William Clissold'.[28] Nor is this merely the growth of critical maturity: as early as 1913 he was writing to Edward Marsh, separating himself from his Georgian contemporaries:

> Poor [W. H.] Davies—he makes me so furious, and so sorry. He's really like a linnet that's got just a wee little sweet song, but it only sings when it's wild. And he's made himself a tame bird.... And now I've got to quarrel with you about the Ralph Hodgson poem: because I think it is banal in utterance.... He takes out his poetic purse, and gives you a handful of cash, and feels very strongly, even a bit sentimentally over it.
>
> —the sky was lit
> The sky was stars all over it,
> I stood, I knew not why.
>
> No one should say 'I knew not why' any more. It is as meaningless as 'yours truly' at the end of a letter.[29]

On Arnold Bennett's *Anna of the Five Towns*—remembering that Bennett was considered the greatest English novelist of the time—we have: 'I hate Bennett's resignation. Tragedy ought really to be a great kick at misery. But *Anna of the Five Towns* seems like an acceptance'.[30] On Compton Mackenzie, another very popular writer then, 'Mackenzie was a fool not to know that the times are too serious to bother about his *Sinister Street* frippery. Folk will either read sheer rubbish, or something that has in it as much or more emotional force than the newspaper has in *it* to-day' (1914).[31] On Lascelles Abercrombie, ranked

[27] *Phoenix*, pp. 322 ff.
[28] *ibid.*, p. 346.
[29] *Letters*, pp. 151 ff.
[30] *ibid.*, p. 64, 1912.
[31] *ibid.*, p. 212 (1914).

as a major poet at the time: 'It is no good your telling me Lascelles' *End of the World* is great, because it isn't. There are some fine bits of rhetoric, as there always are in Abercrombie. But oh, the spirit of the thing altogether seems mean and rather vulgar. . . . I hate and detest his ridiculous imitation yokels and all the silly hash of his bucolics; I loathe his rather nasty efforts at cruelty. . . . I detest his irony with its clap-trap solution of everything being that which it seemeth not.'[32] And on a younger writer's, his friend Aldous Huxley's, novels: 'No, I don't like his books: even if I admire a sort of desperate courage of repulsion and repudiation in them. But again, I feel only half a man writes the books—a sort of precocious adolescent.'[33] Of course, part of his criticism arises from his own view of what the novel should be doing, and is a defence of his own independence; but this is valid criticism too. 'Tell Arnold Bennett', he writes after the appearance of *The Rainbow,* 'that all rules of construction hold good only for novels which are copies of other novels. A book which is not a copy of other books has its own construction, and what he calls faults, he being an old imitator, I call characteristics. I shall repeat till I am grey—when they have as good a work to show, they may make their pronouncements *ex cathedra.* Till then, let them learn decent respect.' But then he adds, with typical ingenuousness, 'Still, I think he is generous.'[34]

But the greatest single piece of criticism occurs in the work, never fully published in his lifetime, on Thomas Hardy. He had been powerfully influenced by Hardy in his youth—the early poems and his first novel, *The White Peacock,* show this clearly enough without needing to read E. T.'s *Memoir*. But he learned later to stand at a distance from Hardy and to detect his flaws. He has a sharp eye for specific weaknesses—he singles out the pig-killing scene

[32] *ibid.,* p. 194 (1914).
[33] *ibid.,* p. 783 (1914).
[34] *ibid.,* p. 295 (1915).

from *Jude the Obscure,* for instance, as Hardy's false way of persuading us to share his contempt for Arabella. But more, he sees why the tragic novels as a whole do not in the end move us as great tragedy should.

> He (Hardy) must select his individual with a definite weakness, a certain coldness of temper, inelastic, a certain inevitable and inconquerable adhesion to the community. This is obvious in Troy, Clym, Tess and Jude. They have . . . as it were, a weak life-flow, so that they cannot break away from the old adhesion, they cannot separate themselves from the mass which bore them, they cannot detach themselves from the common. Therefore they are pathetic rather than tragic figures.[35]

And this is all really because with Hardy

> There is a lack of sternness, there is a hesitating betwixt life and public opinion, which diminishes the Wessex novels from the rank of pure tragedy. It is not so much the eternal, immutable laws of being which are transgressed, it is not that vital life-forces are set in conflict with each other, bringing almost inevitable tragedy. . . . It is, in Wessex, that the individual succumbs to what is in its shallowest, public opinion, in its deepest, the human compact by which we live together, to form community.[36]

But Lawrence also has a fine appreciation of the best in Hardy:

> This is a constant revelation in Hardy's novels; that there exists a great background, vital and vivid, which matters more than the people who move upon it. Against the background of dark, passionate Egdon, of the leafy, sappy passion and sentiment of the woodlands, of the unfathomed stars, is drawn the lesser scheme of lives: *The Return of the Native, The Woodlanders*, or *Two on a Tower*. Upon the vast, incomprehensible pattern of some primal morality greater than ever the human mind can grasp, is drawn the little, pathetic pattern of man's moral life and struggle, pathetic, almost ridiculous. . . . This is the wonder of Hardy's novels,

[35] *Study of Thomas Hardy (Phoenix,* pp. 439 ff).
[36] *ibid.*

and gives them their beauty ... this is the magnificent irony it all contains, the challenge, the contempt.

And yet he concludes that even this is not enough for final greatness:

Whereas in Shakespeare or Sophocles the greater, uncomprehended morality, or fate, is actively transgressed and gives active punishment, in Hardy and Tolstoi the lesser, human morality, the mechanical system is actively transgressed, and holds, and punishes the protagonist, whilst the greater morality is only passively, negatively transgressed ... not taking any active part, having no direct connexion with the protagonist. Oedipus, Hamlet, Macbeth set themselves up against ... the unfathomed moral forces of nature, and out of this unfathomed force comes their death. Whereas Anna Karenina, Eustacia, Tess, Sue and Jude find themselves up against the established system of human government and morality, they cannot detach themselves, and are brought down.... Necessarily painful it was, but they were not at war with God, only with Society.... And the judgement of men killed them, not the judgement of their own souls or the judgement of Eternal God.[37]

We shall return to the *Study of Thomas Hardy* later, since it illuminates much in Lawrence's own method and belief. But these quotations alone are enough to show the penetration of Lawrence's insight into the quality of others' writings.

III. THE THINKER

The question whether the artist or the prophet came first in Lawrence would have been answered emphatically by himself.

This pseudo-philosophy of mine—'polyanalytics', as one of my respected critics might say—is deduced from the novels and poems, not the reverse. The novels and poems come unwatched out of one's pen. And then the absolute need which one has for some sort of satisfactory mental attitude towards oneself and things in general makes one try to abstract some definite conclusions from one's experiences

[37] *ibid.*, p. 419 f.

as a writer and as a man. The novels and the poems are pure passionate experience. These 'polyanalytics' are inferences made afterwards, from the experience.[38]

We can observe this priority actually occurring in the composition of *Lady Chatterley's Lover*. In chapter ix occurs the famous passage about the purpose of novel-writing:

> It is the way our sympathy flows and recoils that really determines our lives. And here lies the vast importance of the novel, properly handled. It can inform and lead into new places the flow of our sympathetic consciousness, and it can lead our sympathy away in recoil from things gone dead. . . . But the novel, like gossip, can also excite spurious sympathies and recoils, mechanical and deadening to the psyche. . . .'[39]

Now, Mr Murry has taken this passage and implied from it, in effect, that *Lady Chatterley* is a deliberate working out of a problem, Lawrence being fully conscious all the time of what he was doing.[40] But the passage just quoted occurs not as a comment on Lawrence's own writing (as it so often appears, when given out of its context) but as a comment on Mrs Bolton's gossip which provides the fodder for Clifford Chatterley's satirical little novels with their 'slightly humorous analysis of people and motives which leaves everything in bits at the end . . . rather like puppies tearing sofa cushions to bits.'[41] Indeed, it is an important element in the story that Sir Clifford was a writer, and popular among the literary coteries; and here Lawrence is contrasting this kind of writing, which really is self-conscious and 'voulu', with the genuine kind. As for *Lady Chatterley* as a whole being 'voulu', being anything but 'pure passionate experience' (even in its third and final version[42]), Lawrence gives the case away in his later vindication of the novel.

[38] *Fantasia of the Unconscious,* Secker, 1923, p. 10, Foreword.
[39] *Lady Chatterley's Lover,* Penguin edition, p. 104.
[40] J. Middleton Murry, *Reminiscences of D. H. Lawrence,* p. 270.
[41] *Lady Chatterley's Lover,* Penguin edition, p. 53.
[42] See p. 106 inf.

> I have been asked many times if I intentionally made Clifford paralysed, if it is symbolic. And literary friends say, it would have been better to have left him whole and potent, and to make the woman leave him nevertheless. As to whether the 'symbolism' is intentional—I don't know.[43] Certainly not in the beginning, when Clifford was created. When I created Clifford and Connie, I had no idea what they were or why they were. They just came, pretty much as they are. But the novel was written, from start to finish, three times. And when I read the first version, I recognized that the lameness of Clifford was symbolic of the paralysis, the deeper emotional or passional paralysis, of most men of his sort and class today. I realized that it was perhaps taking an unfair advantage of Connie, to paralyse him technically. It made it so much more vulgar of her to leave him. Yet the story came as it did, by itself, so I left it alone. Whether we call it symbolism or not, it is, in the sense of its happening, inevitable.[44]

This seems to me not only a very acute analysis of the composition of the novel, but a convincing refutation, if one were needed, of any suggestion that Lawrence wrote his novels to illustrate a theme. Had this been the case he would, in *Lady Chatterley* for instance, have altered the balance to suit the lesson. It is clear that, like all great imaginative artists, the living organism of the novel came first to him, and only later came its significance, its 'purpose'.

But we must not conclude from this that a novel or a poem need have no 'philosophy'. In the Foreword to *Fantasia*, already quoted (p. 13), Lawrence goes on:

> Even art is utterly dependent on philosophy: or if you prefer it, on a metaphysic. The metaphysic or philosophy may not be anywhere very accurately stated, and may be quite unconscious, in the artist, yet it is a metaphysic that governs men at the time, and is by all men more or less compre-

[43] In a letter of 1929 he is more emphatic: 'Yes, the paralysis of Sir Clifford is symbolic—all art is *au fond* symbolic, conscious or unconscious.' And in the first version it is actually stated of Sir Clifford that 'His terrible accident, his paralysis or whatever it was, was really symbolical in him. He was always paralysed, in some part of him' (*Letters*, p. 824).

[44] *A Propos of Lady Chatterley's Lover*, Faber, 1930, p. 94.

> hended, and lived. Men live and see according to some gradually developing and gradually withering vision. . . .

Here, of course, Lawrence is vindicating himself for writing a solemn, semi-philosophical book like *Fantasia,* which he was afraid would not sell—and indeed, for long it did not sell. But what he says is quite consistent with his attitude to his more strictly imaginative work. His constantly reiterated refrain is ' You can't fool the novel '.[45] ' Every novelist who amounts to anything has a philosophy—even Balzac—any novel of importance has a purpose. If only the ' purpose ' be large enough, and not at outs with the passional inspiration. . . . The novel . . . won't let you tell didactic lies, and put them over. . . . It is such a bore that nearly all great novelists have a didactic purpose, otherwise a philosophy, directly opposite to their passional inspiration ' (*ib.*). Virginia Woolf was saying the same thing when she observed, *a propos* of Meredith, ' When philosophy is not consumed in a novel, when we can underline this phrase with a pencil, and cut out that exhortation with a pair of scissors and paste the whole into a system, it is safe to say that there is something wrong with the philosophy or with the novel or with both '.[46] This constitutes the difficulty as well as the greatness of the novel. Elsewhere Lawrence said that it is the novelists and dramatists, and not the poets

> Who have their hardest task in reconciling their metaphysic, their theory of being and knowing, with their living sense of being. Because a novel is a microcosm, and because man in viewing the universe must view it in the light of a theory, therefore every novel must have the background or the structural skeleton of some theory of being, some metaphysic. But the metaphysic must always subserve the artistic purpose beyond the artist's conscious aim. Otherwise the novel becomes a treatise. And the danger is, that a man shall make himself a metaphysic to excuse or cover his own faults

[45] *Reflections on the death of a Porcupine,* p. 106.
[46] Virginia Woolf, *The Common Reader* (Series ii), Hogarth, 1925.

> or failure. . . . Then, having made himself a metaphysic of self-justification, or a metaphysic of self-denial, the novelist proceeds to apply the world to this, instead of applying this to the world.[47]

Not only must the novel have a philosophy behind it, but it must have a morality. But what morality?

> Morality is that delicate, for ever trembling and changing *balance* between me and my circumambient universe, which precedes and accompanies a true relatedness. Now here we see the beauty and the great value of the novel. Philosophy, religion, science, they are all of them busy nailing things down, to get a stable equilibrium. . . . But the novel, no. . . . If you try to nail anything down, in the novel, it either kills the novel, or the novel gets up and walks away with the nail.[48]

This is what Lawrence means when he says, again and again, that 'the essential function of art is moral'.[49] It brings him very close, as we shall see later, to the 'existentialists'; and, indeed, some of them would probably agree that it is the imaginative artist who is most really and exactly the philosopher. 'I am a man and alive', says Lawrence. 'For this reason I am a novelist, and being a novelist, I consider myself superior to the saint, the scientist, the philosopher, and the poet, who are all great masters of different bits of man alive, but never get the whole hog.'[50] And since life is a fluid thing, with no absolutes, the real 'message' of the novel will be to say so by its very structure and inner character. 'Let us have done with the ugly imperialism of any absolute. There is no absolute good, there is nothing absolutely right. All things flow and change, and even change is not absolute. The whole is a strange assembly of incongruous parts, slipping past one another.'[51]

[47] *Study of Thomas Hardy* (*Phoenix*, p. 479).
[48] *Morality and the Novel*, 1925. (*Phoenix*, p. 330).
[49] D. H. Lawrence, *Studies in Classical American Literature*, p. 170.
[50] *Why the Novel Matters* (*Phoenix*, p. 536).
[51] *ibid.*

Again we are reminded of Virginia Woolf: 'Life is not a series of gig lamps symmetrically arranged; life is a luminous halo, a semi-transparent envelope surrounding us from the beginning of consciousness to the end. . . .' [52]

We shall see later the danger and the virtue of this 'fluid' conception of life. But given that that is what life *is*, I think we must allow that Lawrence expressed in his art what philosophically he believed; that he reached that point in imaginative being at which the preacher and the poet coincide, since the poem *is* the sermon. And it is significant that for that point of coincidence in the past he refers us to the Bible.

> The books of the Old Testament, Genesis, Exodus, Samuel, Kings, by authors whose purpose was so big, it didn't quarrel with their passionate inspiration. The purpose and the inspiration were almost one. Why, in the name of everything bad the two ever should have got separated, is a mystery! But in the modern novel they are hopelessly divorced.[53]

Some of the 'existentialist' philosophers—Sartre, Marcel, Jaspers, Heidegger—have turned to the poem, the drama or the novel as the places where the speculative intellect may find its living material. But as early as 1923 we find Lawrence saying the same thing when discussing the future of the novel in a very penetrating article for the *International Book Review:*

> If you wish to look into the past for 'what-next' books, you can go back to the Greek philosophers. Plato's Dialogues are queer little novels. It seems to me it was the greatest pity in the world when philosophy and fiction got split. They used to be one, right from the days of the myth. Then they went and parted, like a nagging married couple, with Aristotle and Thomas Aquinas and that beastly Kant. So the novel went sloppy, and philosophy went abstract-dry. The two should come together again—in the novel.[54]

[52] Virginia Woolf, *The Common Reader* (Series i), *The Novel.*
[53] *Porcupine,* p. 108.
[54] *Phoenix,* p. 520.

CHAPTER TWO

THE DEATH OF A SON

I

WHATEVER our assessment of the individual novels of Lawrence or of his work as a whole, we cannot deny that his influence upon English fiction in the twentieth century has been as great as any of his contemporaries. That influence has not been, perhaps, so direct as some: an influence upon actual technique or preoccupation, such as the influence of Virginia Woolf or of an earlier writer who did not begin to affect the English novelist until the 'thirties, Franz Kafka. Rather it has been an influence of negation, in some ways like that of James Joyce (though Joyce had his direct influence as well, of course). That is to say, he has not compelled his successors to write like him, but he has made it impossible for them to write like his own predecessors. We have seen, in the last chapter, something of the acuteness of his perception into the Georgian literary scene. We must now look at this more closely and see how that perception came to dictate his own approach.

The quotations given in the last chapter show Lawrence seeing through the usual plot-cum-character technique of Bennett and the rest. The sense that something was wrong there was reinforced by the conviction that he had something different to do himself. His first three novels, *The White Peacock, The Trespasser* and *Sons and Lovers* were written still more or less in the old idiom. But when he begins to be big with what will ultimately be *The Rainbow,* he has a feeling that now something very decisive is happening within him. The first warning was in a letter to Edward Garnett in 1913: 'I have done 100 pages of a novel. I think you will hate it.... It is quite different in manner from my other stuff—far less visualized. It is what I *can* write just now, and write with pleasure.... And it is good too.' [1] And as he grows more convinced of its rightness, he can write again, a month later, 'I've written rather more than half of a most fascinating (to me) novel. But nobody will ever dare to publish it.... I love and adore this new book. It's all crude as yet... but I think it's great—so new, so really a stratum deeper than I think anybody has ever gone, in a novel.' [2] What was the new thing he had discovered, which appears in *The Rainbow* and its sequel, *Women in Love?* We shall have to quote again the often quoted letter to Garnett, outlining what he felt. Replying to Garnett's criticism, he says:

> I don't think the psychology is wrong: it is only that I have a different attitude to my characters, and that necessitates a different attitude in you, which you are not prepared to give.... Somehow—that which is physic—non-human, in humanity is more interesting to me than the old-fashioned human element—which causes one to conceive a character in a certain moral scheme and make him consistent. The certain moral scheme is what I object to.... I don't so much care about what the woman *feels*—in the ordinary usage of the word. That presumes an *ego* to feel with. I only care about what the woman *is*—what she IS—inhumanly, physiologically, materially.... You mustn't look in my novel for the old stable *ego* of the character. There is another *ego*, according to whose action the individual is unrecognizable, and passes through, as it were, allotropic states which it needs a deeper sense than any we've been used to exercise, to discover are states of the same single radically unchanged element.... The characters fall into the form of some other rhythmic form, as when one draws a fiddle-bow across a fine tray delicately sanded, the sand takes lines unknown.[3]

[1] *Letters,* p. 105.
[2] *ibid.,* p. 111.
[3] *ibid.,* pp. 197 ff.

Here we have two elements intermingling. The first is an impatience with personality, and I think that at first he is here reacting against the 'cult of personality'; later this develops (1915) into the extremes of

> I am tired of this insistence on the *personal* element; personal truth, personal reality. It is very stale and profitless. I want some new non-personal activity, which is at the same time a genuine vital activity. And I want relations which are not purely personal, based on purely personal qualities; but relations based upon some unanimous accord in truth or belief, and a harmony of *purpose*, rather than of personality.[4]

The second element which intermingles with the first is his developing religion of the blood. It is important to realize that this religion was already there, in embryo, at the time of *Sons and Lovers*. This can be seen from the curious Foreword he wrote to that novel, which was never published with it but only published later in the *Letters*.[5] And even before the publication of *Sons and Lovers*, we find him writing, in 1913:

> My great religion is a belief in the blood, the flesh, as being wiser than the intellect. We can go wrong in our minds. But what our blood feels and believes and says is always true. . . . That is why I like to live in Italy. The people are so unconscious.[6]

Indeed, we can even see glimmerings of it in his very first novel. It has often been pointed out that the gamekeeper, Annable, in *The White Peacock* (1911), is a foreshadowing of Mellors, the gamekeeper in *Lady Chatterley*—Annable, the ex-parson, come down in the world but now established in a contented, mindless condition with the motto 'be a good animal, true to your animal instinct'. But Annable is soon killed in the quarry; it is upon George that the novel centres. And in the presentation of George's physique, of the relationship between him and Cyril (the 'I' of the novel,

[4] *ibid.*, p. 289.
[5] *ibid.*, pp. 95-102.
[6] *ibid.*, p. 94.

in fact, Lawrence himself, though he is less obtrusive than in any other novel into which the author himself enters), of the accord between him and the farm, there is an anticipation of what will develop in the later novels.

> The cool, moist fragrance of the morning, the intentional stillness of everything, of the tall bluish trees, of the wet, frank flowers, of the trustful moths folded and unfolded in the fallen swaths, was a perfect medium of sympathy. The horses moved with a still dignity, obeying his commands.[7]

But we can sense the immaturity. George ends as a drunkard, and his slow decay, though moving, is not genuinely tragic. There is some brilliant writing.

> I sat by my window and watched the low clouds reel and stagger past. It seemed as if everything were being swept along—I myself seemed to have lost my substance, to have become detached from concrete things and the firm trodden pavement of every-day life. Onward, always onward, not knowing where, nor why, the wind, the clouds, the rain and the birds and the leaves, everything whirling along—why? . . . The crow looked at me—I was certain he looked at me. 'What do you think of it all?' I asked him.

Note the conversation with the bird—we shall have plenty of that later. But note also the early manner, and the trick which later he will see through in the Georgian poets. ('No one should say, "I know not why" any more. It is as meaningless as "yours truly" at the end of a letter', *Letters,* p. 151.)

In *Sons and Lovers* (1913) there are similar glimpses of what is to come, but on the whole not with approval. There is Paul's relationship with Clara, for instance:

> He felt more and more that his experience had been impersonal, and not Clara. He loved her. There was a big tenderness, as after a strong emotion they had known together; but it was not she who could keep his soul steady. . . . To know their own nothingness, to know the tremendous

[7] *The White Peacock,* p. 134.

> living flood which carried them always, gave them rest within themselves. If so great a magnificent power could overwhelm them, identify them altogether with itself, so that they knew they were only grains in the tremendous heave that lifted every grass-blade its little height, and every tree, and living thing, then why fret about themselves? [8]

But what was true at the beginning of their love-affair does not remain true. At one time

> The emotion was strong enough to carry with it everything—reason, soul, blood—in a great sweep, like the Trent carries bodily its back-swirls and intertwinings, noiselessly. Gradually the little criticisms, the little sensations, were lost, thought also went, everything borne along in one flood. He became, not a man with a mind, but a great instinct . . . It was as if he, and the stars, and the dark herbage, and Clara were licked up in an immense tongue of flame, which tore onwards and upwards.[9]

But it is not enough. Clara complains: ' It seems . . . as if you only loved me at night—as if you didn't love me in the daytime '.[10] Later on, when Lawrence has rejected ' love ', in the usual sense, this love-in-darkness *will* be enough. But at present it will not do; and Clara returns to her husband, Baxter Dawes, who, unsatisfactory person though he is, knows how to give all of himself. How, then, did Lawrence—in person, and in his novels—come to achieve the shift of emphasis? The answer is: through the death of his Mother, and the gradual death of Paul Morel, her son.

II

In a letter to Garnett about *Sons and Lovers* in 1912 [11] Lawrence describes the novel and says that the hero of it ' is left in the end naked of everything, with the drift

[8] *Sons and Lovers,* p. 377.
[9] *ibid.,* p. 382.
[10] *ibid.,* p. 382.
[11] *Letters,* pp. 76 ff.

towards death'. Now this is interesting. For from the last pages of the novel itself we should not have gained quite that impression. True, much of Paul is still bound to his dead mother—as we see from the rather maudlin poem 'The Virgin Mother':[12]

And so, my love, my mother,
I shall always be true to you.
Twice I am born, my dearest,
To life, and to death, in you;
And this is the life hereafter
Wherein I am true...

Is the last word now uttered
Is the farewell said?
Spare me the strength to leave you
Now you are dead.
I must go, but my soul lies helpless
Beside your bed.

But by the time he actually comes to write the last paragraphs of the novel he has stepped a little further out of Paul Morel:

> His soul could not leave her, wherever she was. Now she was gone abroad into the night and he was with her still. They were together... 'Mother!' he whispered—'mother'.... But no, he would not give in. Turning sharply, he walked towards the city's phosphorescence. His fists were shut, his mouth set fast. He would not take that direction, to the darkness, to follow her. He walked towards the faintly humming, glowing town, quickly.

It is really Miriam who has the 'drift towards death'. As they go out of his room, to part for ever:

> How bitter, how unutterably bitter, it made her that he rejected her sacrifice! Life ahead looked dead, as if the glow were gone out.... She waited for him, took the flowers, and they went out together, he talking, she feeling dead.

Writers on Lawrence have, it seems to me, much exaggerated his Oedipus complex. The mother-attachment once shaken off, Paul Morel once dead, he does grow into a

[12] *Amores* (written 1916).

separate existence which cannot be interpreted in terms of Mrs Lawrence. True, there are occasional echoes of it later. It recurs again, for instance, at Miss Frost's death in *The Lost Girl:* 'Alvina knew death—which is untellable. She knew that her darling carried away a portion of her own soul into death.'[13] But this is only faint. Had it been stronger it would surely have appeared in *The Rainbow* and its sequel, where there would have been plenty of scope for a 'Mrs Morel-Paul' theme. But whereas there are hints of the relationship between Lawrence's father and mother in Tom Brangwen and Lydia Lensky (Lydia's first marriage to the Pole has an echo of Mrs Lawrence's first love before she met the father of D. H.), there is very little of the possessive motherhood anywhere. In the superb first three chapters of *The Rainbow* (among the greatest Lawrence ever wrote) there is the search for—and discovery of—a satisfactory relationship such as the Morel-Lawrence family lacked. Tom and Lydia come and go in their love, but finally come back together in a completion which we do not find achieved anywhere else in the novels, unless perhaps in *The Lost Girl* (in *Lady Chatterley* we are promised it, but can hardly expect it). And in that completion the girl Anna, at first suspicious of her stepfather, is put at peace:

> She looked from one to the other, and she saw them established to her safety, and she was free. She played between the pillar of fire and the pillar of cloud in confidence, having the assurance on her right hand and the assurance on her left. She was no longer called upon to uphold with her childish might the broken end of the arch. Her father and her mother now met to the span of the heavens, and she, the child, was free to play in the space beneath, between.[14]

Mr Horace Gregory rightly picks on the Cathedral (Lincoln) as the central symbol of *The Rainbow*.[15] In *Sons and Lovers* Paul takes his mother to Lincoln.

[13] *The Lost Girl,* p. 60.
[14] *The Rainbow,* p. 88.
[15] H. Gregory, *Pilgrim of the Apocalypse,* Secker, 1934.

> They saw the great Cathedral lying couchant above the plain. . . . He looked at his mother. Her blue eyes were watching the cathedral quietly. She seemed again to be beyond him. Something in the eternal repose of the uplifted cathedral, blue and noble against the sky, was reflected in her, something of the fatality.

But Paul is becoming bitter, and when they go into the Cathedral, and his mother's face becomes joyful and peaceful in the service, ' all the time he was wanting to rage and smash things and cry '.[16] In *The Rainbow* the Cathedral calls forth a similar antagonism, but it is in the opposite direction. It is Will Brangwen who is satisfied, but Anna who is disturbed.

> His soul leapt, soared up into the great church . . . into the gloom, into possession, it reeled, it swooned with a great escape, it quivered in the womb, in the hush and the gloom of fecundity. . . . Containing birth and death, potential with all the noise and transitation of life, the cathedral remained hushed, a great involved seed, whereof the flower would be radiant life inconceivable, but whose beginning and whose end were the circle of silence. Spanned round with the rainbow, the jewelled gloom folded music upon silence, light upon darkness, fecundity upon death, as a seed folds leaf upon leaf and silence upon the root and the flower, hushing up the secret of all between its parts, the death out of which it fell, the life into which it has dropped, the immortality it involves, and the death it will embrace again. Here in the church, ' before ' and ' after ' were folded together, all was contained in a oneness.[17]

Readers of Mr Eliot's *Four Quartets* can hardly help recalling the symbol of the rose, into which the tongues of flame are in-folded and towards which time before and time after point their way. Here is perhaps Lawrence's most sympathetic statement, and rejection, of the classic, Catholic scheme. For Will had turned away from Absolute Beauty, and ' turned to the Gothic form, which always asserted the

[16] *Sons and Lovers,* pp. 257 ff.
[17] *The Rainbow,* p. 189.

broken desire of mankind in its pointed arches, escaping the rolling, absolute beauty of the round arch '.[18] Whereas Anna only loved the Cathedral ' as a world not her own'; for ' after all, there was the sky outside . . . the open sky was no blue vault, no dark dome hung with many twinkling lamps, but a space where stars were wheeling in freedom, with freedom above them always higher '.[19] Yet in spite of this conflict, Anna and Will do not go apart. Anna sinks into her family, her children (five of them), and Will rediscovers sensual activity—in her and in carpentry. It is left to their daughter, Ursula, to work out their restlessness to the full. After first love, the homosexual relationship with Winifred Inger, and the hard, maturing experience as a teacher (Lawrence knew it), she is left still undiscovered by herself.

> That which she was, positively, was dark and unrevealed, it could not come forth. It was like a seed buried in dry ash. . . . This lighted area, lit up by man's completest consciousness, she thought was all the world: that here all was disclosed for ever. Yet all the time, within the darkness she had been aware of points of light, like the eyes of wild beasts, gleaming, penetrating, vanishing. . . . This inner circle of light in which she lived and moved, wherein trains rushed . . . and the plants and the animals worked by the light of science and knowledge, suddenly it seemed like the area under an arc-lamp, wherein the moths and children played in the security of blinding light, not even knowing there was any darkness, because they stayed in the light.[20]

She still has terrible experiences to undergo—the disillusionment with Anton Skrebensky, the nightmare of an encounter with horses in the rain, and the miscarriage of a child by Anton. But at the end of the novel the Cathedral-arch becomes a rainbow-arch, and she begins at last to move out of the narrow circle of science and knowledge towards the promise of the future:

[18] *ibid.*, p. 222.
[19] *ibid.*, pp. 189 ff.
[20] *ibid.*, p. 418.

> She knew that the sordid people who crept hard-scaled and separate on the face of the world's corruption were living still, that their rainbow was arched in their blood and would quiver to life in their spirit, that they would cast off their horny covering of disintegration, that new clean, naked bodies would issue to a new germination, to a new growth, rising to the light and the wind and the clean rain of heaven. She saw in the rainbow the earth's new architecture, the old, brittle corruption of houses and factories swept away, the world built up in a living fabric of Truth, fitting to the over-arching heaven.[21]

III

If *The Rainbow* gave chances of pursuing the 'Mrs Morel-Paul' theme, still more did *Women in Love*. For here Ursula and Gudrun both get married against their parents' will. But Will Brangwen and Anna are only faintly seen in the background of Ursula's life and there is nothing left of the brilliant, intrinsic life they both possessed in *The Rainbow*. It is not quite true to say, as Horace Gregory does, that 'the narrative link between the novels is patently artificial, the Brangwen family name is used . . . but the characters of Ursula and Gudrun are not logical developments of the young women who held the centre of attention in the last pages of *The Rainbow*. They are new creations and their names are arbitrary.' For in *The Rainbow* Ursula, after learning of Anton's marriage, says to herself wearily and repeatedly: 'I have no father nor mother nor lover, I have no allocated place in the world of things, I do not belong to Beldover nor to Nottingham nor to England nor to this world, they none of them exist, I am trammelled and entangled in them, but they are all unreal. I must break out of it, like a nut from its shell which is unreality.'[22] And surely the Ursula of *Women in Love* is but a development of this. But it is true that the focus of Lawrence's attention

[21] *ibid.*, p. 467.
[22] *ibid.*, p. 464.

has so shifted that the Brangwen parents do not seem to be the same people. And not only the Brangwen parents, but everybody else, except for the four main characters, is only seen faintly in the background. The people who gather at the Critch's are all—except Hermione, who is known to have been based on Lady Ottoline Morrel—quite unreal. Even the drowning of Diana Critch and young Mr Brindell has none of the vividness of other water scenes in Lawrence—the flood at the Marsh which drowns Tom, the breaking of the sluice in *The Virgin and the Gipsy*, etc. It seems to have been inserted, not for its own sake, but to give an occasion for Birkin's musings about death:

> I don't mind about the dead once they are dead. The worst of it is, they cling to the living and won't let go. . . . There is life which belongs to death, and there is life which isn't death. One is tired of the life that belongs to death—our kind of life. . . . Love is like sleep, like death—I *do* want to die from this life—and yet it is more than life itself. . . .[23]

It is significant that at this point, where the old vivid description of events seems momentarily to have lost its bite, there emerges the problem which from now on will, consciously or unconsciously, obsess Lawrence—the problem which obsesses all 'existentialist' philosophers too: the problem of speech. Ursula is listening to Birkin's musings about death:

> She listened, making out what he said. She knew, as well as he knew, that words themselves do not convey meaning, that they are but a gesture we make, a dumb show like any other. And she seemed to feel his gesture through her blood, and she drew back. . . . He turned in confusion. There was always confusion in speech. Yet it must be spoken. Whichever way one moved, if one were to move forwards, one must break a way through. . . .

Lawrence recognized well enough the paradox—that a writer should have to use words to talk about the inade-

[23] *Women in Love*, p. 152.

quacy of words. ' I'm like Carlyle ', he once wrote, ' who, they say, wrote 50 volumes on the value of silence.'[24] But like any real writer, he had to hack his way through the jungle of words by means of a verbal hatchet, and it is at this stage that he is learning to penetrate the densest part of it.

This will, I think, explain what appears to many as the failure of *Women in Love*. They complain that the characters are undifferentiated and unrecognizable; and this is frequently true. The whole novel is, as we have seen in the letter to Garnett quoted earlier in this chapter (p. 44 *sup.*), precisely an attempt to do without differentiated characters, or at least—since that would be absurd—with the minimum of differentiation. Birkin even says:

> I abhor humanity, I wish it was swept away. It could go, and there would be no *absolute* loss, if every human being perished tomorrow. . . . Don't you find it a beautiful clean thought, a world empty of people, just uninterrupted grass, and a hare sitting up? . . . Man is one of the mistakes of creation—like the ichthyosauri. If only he were gone again, think what lovely things would come out of the liberated days;—things straight out of the fire.[25]

Of course Birkin is in an extreme mood when he says this. But Lawrence is here starting off on his search for the ' dark Gods ', beyond knowledge and beyond man. Horace Gregory is right to select the carved West African figure as an important symbol of this novel. In *The Rainbow* Anton had brought Ursula a momentary glimpse of Africa (the one country, curiously enough, that Lawrence himself never got to):

> In a low, vibrating voice he told her about Africa, the strange darkness, the strange, blood fear. . . . In Africa it seems massive (the darkness) and fluid with terror—not fear of anything—just fear. One breathes it, like a smell of blood.[26]

[24] *Letters* (1913), p. 95.
[25] *Women in Love*, pp. 102 ff.
[26] *The Rainbow*, p. 421.

But it is here, in *Women in Love,* that Africa really looms out of the darkness. They are admiring some statues, wood-carvings (' from the West Pacific ', as Lawrence wrongly states), and at one in particular: Birkin remarks that ' There are centuries and hundred of centuries of development in a straight line, behind that carving; it is an awful pitch of culture, of a definite sort '. Later in the novel, after the strange scene in which Ursula sees Birkin fiercely throwing stones at the moon's reflection on the pond, there is a reminiscence of this statue.

> He knew he did not want a further sensual experience. He remembered the . . . statuette about two feet high, a tall, slim, elegant figure from West Africa, in dark wood, glossy and suave. It was a woman, with hair dressed high, like a melon-shaped dome. . . . She knew what he himself did not know. . . . Thousands of years ago, that which was imminent in himself must have taken place in these Africans: the goodness, the holiness, the desire for creation and productive happiness, must have lapsed, leaving the single impulse for knowledge in one sort, mindless progressive knowledge through the senses, knowledge arrested and ending in the senses, mystic knowledge in disintegration and dissolution . . .[27]

Birkin contrasts to himself the Northern, white races, who, ' having the arctic north behind them, the vast abstraction of ice and snow, would fulfil a mystery of ice-destructive knowledge, snow-abstract annihilation '. Whether it is deliberate or not, it is significant (as Stephen Potter[28] and Horace Gregory point out) that Gerald, the typical northern white, is as a matter of fact killed in the snows of Switzerland. Birkin on the other hand does find a genuine fulfilment when Ursula finally accepts him on his own terms. And from then on the language describing their relation is full of ' resurrection ' imagery.

> He received her into his soul . . . he, who was so nearly dead, who was so near to being gone with the rest of his race down

[27] *ibid.,* p. 210.
[28] Stephen Potter, *D. H. Lawrence: a First Study,* Cape, 1930.

> the slope of mechanical death.... This marriage with her was his resurrection and his life.[29]

And she too:

> She was with Birkin, she had just come to life, here in the high snow, against the stars. What had she to do with parents and antecedents? She knew herself new and unbegotten, she had no father, no mother, no anterior connections, she was herself, pure and silvery, she belonged to the oneness with Birkin, a oneness that struck deeper notes, sounding into the heart of the universe... where she had never existed before.[30]

Horace Gregory says of *Women in Love* that ' the four important people in the novel are scarcely human beings at all but seem to be gigantic personifications of the sex act. ....Ursula might well be Gudrun or Gudrun Ursula, and the two men, Gerald and Birkin, seem to intermingle in the same fashion.' This is not always so: there is a clear difference all along between the love-making of Ursula and Birkin, ending in marriage, and that of Gudrun and Gerald, ending in a liaison, followed by Gerald's death and by Gudrun's pursuit into Germany of the unlikely Loerke. But it is true that, apart from the actual sexual relationship, there is very little differentiation between the sisters—who are good friends—or between Birkin and Gerald—who are blood-brothers. It is perhaps significant of a certain awareness of failure in the case of Gerald that Lawrence brings him to life again—or someone very like him with the same name—in his play, *Touch and Go* (1919), where he tries to picture him in a more achieved relationship with a woman. But the play is a failure as the novel is not.

For genuine appreciation of the novel we have not only to read it two or three times; but we have also to try to understand what it is Lawrence is attempting to do. It is almost incredible, for instance, that it was this novel—of all Lawrence's the least ' picturesque '—about which there were negotiations in Hollywood some ten years later for a

[29] *Women in Love,* p. 309.
[30] *ibid.,* p. 342.

possible film.[31] (In any case, Lawrence loathed the cinema, as we can see from the remarks of Mr May in *The Lost Girl;* and the Brewsters record that when, to pass the time, he went one day with them to see *Ben Hur,* he nearly vomited in the cinema, and they all went out before the end.[32]) The project of a film of *Women in Love*—not unnaturally—never came off; but Lawrence does not seem to have been violently opposed to the idea. It is certain in any case that the cinema probably could not and undoubtedly would not have been able to express Lawrence's insight into the realms 'beyond personality'. Later on (1921) Lawrence is to apply the same insight to a very different subject—the teaching of history. In the Introduction to his (little-known) *Movements in European History*[33] he says:

> Unfortunately nothing is more difficult than to re-create the *personal* reality of a bygone age. Personality is local and temporal. Each age has its own. And each age proceeds to interpret every other age in terms of the current personality. So that Shakespeare's Caesar is an Elizabethan, and Bernard Shaw's is a Victorian, and neither of them is Caesar. The *personal* Caesar we shall never know. But there is some eternal, impersonal Caesar whom we *can* know, historically. . . . The present small book is an attempt to give some impression of the great, surging movements which rose in the hearts of men in Europe, sweeping them apart for ever on the tides of opposition. These are movements which have no deducible origin. They have no reasonable cause, though they are so great that we must call them impersonal. . . . It is all beyond reasonable cause and effect, though these may be deduced later. It is all outside personality, though it makes personality. It is greater than any one man, though in individual men the power is at its greatest. . . . All that the reason can do, in discovering such passion (*e.g.*, as that which gave rise to the Reformation) and its effects, afterwards, is to realize that life *was* so, mysteriously, creatively, beyond cavil.

[31] Knud Merrild, *A Poet and Two Painters,* pp. 124, 128.
[32] E. and A. Brewster, *Reminiscences and Correspondence of D. H. Lawrence,* p. 298.
[33] 'Lawrence H. Davison', *Movements in European History,* OUP, 1921.

I have given that quotation at length because it is unfamiliar and because it happens to be one of the best expositions I know of what Lawrence was after—of what he was beginning to be after in *Women in Love*. The weaknesses of this novel are clear enough, but they do not seem to me to lie where most people locate them. It is not so much the lack of visual reality, for that is there when Lawrence really needs it. It is the fact that frequently the symbols, the pegs of incident, are not stout enough, so to speak, to bear the weight of comment and conclusion that is hung upon them. The scene, for instance, in chapter eight where Hermione, in fierce hatred of Birkin, brings down a heavy glass ball on his head is so emotionally melodramatic as to be almost comic; and it is made no better by Birkin's odd reaction in going out of the house to the hills and sitting naked among the primroses and then masochistically moving up and down among the bristles of the fir-boughs. But when the style escapes from its frequent tendency to a cloying kind of over-chargedness, the novel does succeed amazingly in exploring regions of human consciousness which could never be actually described, and can only be indicated by this very method which Lawrence here devises. Part of Lawrence's emancipation from the superficies of 'personality' is Lawrence's own emancipation from his mother. It is true that he can still think of her, many years after, in Taos. But how differently:

> England seems full of graves to me,
> Full of graves.
>
> Women I loved and cherished, like my mother;
> Yet I had to tell them to die. . . .
>
> So now I whisper: Come away,
> Come away from the place of graves, come west,
> Women,
> Women whom I loved and told to die.[34]

[34] *Spirits Summoned West,* from *Ghosts,* Collected Poems, vol. 1, Secker, 1928.

And he remarked once to the Brewsters that he felt like rewriting *Sons and Lovers:* he had not done justice there, he said, to his father—' a clean-cut, and exuberant spirit, a true pagan '—and he now blamed his mother for her self-righteousness.[35]

Indeed, in his poetry Lawrence often seems to fail to achieve the severance from ' personality ' that he is striving for in his prose. In the note to the 1929 Collected Edition of his poems he makes a significant claim. ' It seems to me that no poetry, not even the best, should be judged as if it existed in the absolute, in the vacuum of the absolute. Even the best poetry, when it is at all personal, needs the penumbra of its own time and place and circumstance to make it full and whole.' He instances Shakespeare's *Sonnets;* and he asks the reader to make the same filling-in for his own poems of ' *Look! We Have Come Through!* ' Of course there is a truth in this; but it can easily give rise to the ' personal heresy ' in literature. And in the poems it seems to me that Lawrence does often ruin the poetry by the intrusion of his personal problems. We have quoted one bad poem above (p. 48); here is another, where a promise of vividness is destroyed by a personal stridency:

> Nevertheless the curse against you is still in my heart
> Like a deep, deep burn.
> The curse against all mothers who fortify themselves in
> motherhood, devastating the vision . . .
> It burns within me like a deep, old burn,
> And oh, I wish it were better.[36]

We can see it even more clearly in the ' Ballad of a Wilful Woman ', where an imaginary scene during the Flight from Egypt is charmingly, and with a gentle blasphemy, depicted. It starts so well, with good, light ballad verse:

[35] E. and A. Brewster, *Reminiscences and Correspondence of D. H. Lawrence,* p. 254.
[36] *She Looks Back* from *Look! We Have Come Through* (1917), pub. in *Collected Poems,* vol. ii.

She has given the child to Joseph,
Gone down to the flashing shore;
And Joseph, shading his eyes with his hand,
Stands watching evermore.

But after a bit the Blessed Virgin becomes, only too obviously, Frieda, Joseph becomes the Nottingham Professor, and the man whom Mary goes after is Lawrence; and then we get a decline in the *quality* of the verse itself:

She follows his restless wanderings
Till night when, by the fire's red stain,
Her face is bent, in the bitter stream
That comes from the flowers of pain. . . .

We shall see below (page 94) that the same danger sometimes threatens his prose. (It is especially threatening in some parts of *Aaron's Rod,* a great deal of *Kangaroo,* and some of *The Plumed Serpent.*) But on the whole it is worked off most usefully in his poetry, which thus becomes a safety-valve for what might damage his novels—this is why Lawrence, in spite of occasional things of considerable beauty and perception, is not a great poet.[37] And it is at this stage in his life, the stage discussed in this chapter, that the verse happens to be the most frequent dumping-ground. It is *Women in Love,* together with its predecessor, that marks the real development in Lawrence's art. Along with the death of the Mother, Paul Morel, a Mother's son, has too to die, before the greatest Lawrence can be born.

[37] For a contradiction of this view, see a fine essay, 'D. H. Lawrence: The Single State of Man' by Mr A. Alvarez in *A D. H. Lawrence Miscellany* (ed. Harry T. Moore: Heinemann, 1961).

CHAPTER THREE

ENGLAND, MY ENGLAND!

I

At last came death, sufficiency of death,
and that at last relieved me, I died.
I buried my beloved; it was good, I buried myself and
was gone.
War came and every hand raised to murder....
Very good, very good, I am a murderer! ...
and I am dead, trodden to nought in the smoke-sodden
tomb:
dead and trodden to nought in the sour black earth.

(1915: 'New Heaven and New Earth'
—from *Look! We Have Come Through!*)

In the autobiographical chapter, called 'The Nightmare', in *Kangaroo,* Richard Lovat Somers (Lawrence) is described as 'one of the most intensely English little men England had ever produced, with a passion for his country, even if it were often a passion of hatred'. This note is specifically introduced, of course, to stress the absurdity of the authorities in Cornwall for suspecting him and Harriet (Frieda) of being spies, and ordering them to leave their house at Zennor in October, 1917. The whole story is told —and it is an absurd one—in the *Letters* and in this autobiographical chapter. But already earlier in the war he had written in tones of sadness which also revealed a deep affection for England:

> It seems as if we were all going to be dragged into the *danse macabre*. One can only grin, and be fatalistic. My dear nation is bitten by the tarantula, and the venom has gone home at last.... It is very sad, but one isn't sad any more. It is ...

no use crying over spilt milk.... The poor dear ship of Christian democracy is scuttled at last, the breach is made, the veil of the temple is torn, our epoch is over.[1]

It is true that Lawrence often affects to despise his country or at least to regard it as merely a convenience. He was frankly relieved when declared unfit for military service in the 1914–18 war, although he always made it clear that he was not a conscientious objector. He says, for instance:

> All this war, this talk of nationality, to me is false. I *feel* no nationality, not fundamentally. I feel no passion for my land, nor my own house, nor my own furniture, nor my own money. Therefore I won't pretend any.
>
> You are quite right, I do esteem individual liberty above everything. What is a nation for, but to secure the maximum of liberty to every individual? What do you think a nation *is*?—a big business concern? What is the *raison d'être* of a nation—to produce wealth? How horrible! A nation is a number of people united to secure the maximum amount of liberty for each member of that nation, and to fulfil collectively the highest truth known to them.[2]

But these remarks are rather superficial, thrown out in war-time correspondence and controversy. We can discern his deeper feelings by watching his treatment of England in the novels, and his emotional reaction to separation from England. Looking back more calmly in 1918, when he was making a study of classic American writers, he could say, in words now famous though they will bear repetition:

> Every continent has its own great spirit of place. Every people is polarized in some particular locality, which is home, the homeland. Different places on the face of the earth have different vital effluence, different vibration, different chemical exhalation, different polarity with different stars: call it what you like. But the spirit of place is a great reality. The Nile produced not only the corn, but the terrific religions of Egypt.... The Island of Great Britain had a wonderful terrestrial magnetism or polarity of its own, which made the

[1] *Letters* (1916), p. 346.
[2] *ibid.*, p. 356.

> British people. For the moment, this polarity seems to be breaking. Can England die? And what if England dies? [3]

As soon after the first Great War as possible Lawrence got away from England, and from now on his travels started. His bad treatment by the military powers in Cornwall undoubtedly shook his faith in England severely. His letters show him quite calm and self-controlled about it, but the wound still rankled in 1922 when he came to write *Kangaroo,* with its autobiographical chapter describing the episode. It is important, however, to remember that the flight from England was a flight from more than his native land—his native land which he loved but which had first snubbed him by confiscating copies of *The Rainbow,* then (understandably) failed to support him as a writer during the war, and finally crowned it by the farcical suspicion of alien activity. In the 'Argument' he wrote for the volume of poems called *Look! We Have Come Through!* (commenced in 1912, but mostly post-war) he thus describes its provenance:

> After much struggling and loss in love and in the world of man, the protagonist throws in his lot with a woman who is already married. Together they go into another country, she perforce leaving her children behind. The conflict of love and hate goes on between the man and the woman, and between these two and the world around them, till it reaches some sort of conclusion.

He is referring, of course, also to earlier visits to the Continent, and to the whole long episode of his marriage with Frieda and disentangling of her from her three children. But it is clear that they did not 'come through' finally until the war was over and they could set off to explore other lands.

The Lost Girl—written in Sicily in 1920 and published the same year—is the first major work that comes from this exile. Before that he had only published poems, short stories and descriptive articles, since writing *Women in Love*

[3] *Studies in Classical American Literature,* p. 12.

(though this last was not published till 1921). Dr Leavis rather surprisingly once called it 'his best *novel*'—'novel' italicized to indicate that other works of his may be greater but are less successful as novels. But there are indications that Lawrence himself thought of *The Lost Girl* as—in parts, at least—something of a pot-boiler. 'I think it's quite amusing: and quite moral', he wrote; and 'Let's hope my *Lost Girl* will be *Treasure Trove* to me. . . . One must make money these days; or perish'.[4] More serious is the internal evidence of half-heartedness. The most obvious characteristic of it is that it does not really come alive until chapter fourteen, 'The Journey Across'. True, Cicio has already fascinated us earlier, creeping around in his uneasy, Italian way, a fish out of water in England. But Lawrence has in the first half—or rather, two-thirds—of the novel produced an almost Dickensian profusion of characters, none of whom he is for long interested in, except Alvina herself. Her father, James Houghton, together with Miss Frost and Miss Pinnegar (not to mention the shadowy Mrs Houghton, who is scarcely visible at all) are only there to show the drift of middle-class England towards stagnation. Only for one moment, when she goes down a mine with her father and is shown round by a nameless miner (another embryo Mellors of *Lady Chatterley*), does something of the real Lawrentian penetration appear. Nor is this due to the by-passing of personality, as in *Women in Love;* for Lawrence is clearly interested in the queer little theatrical troup, the 'Natch-Kee-Tawaras', a sort of cosmopolitan *Good Companions*. Moreover there are occasional tell-tale signs, such as we shall have to point out in *Aaron's Rod,* in the actual mechanics of the story-telling. 'Surely enough books have been written about heroines in similar circumstances', he writes, of Alvina's time of hospital-training; 'there is no need to go into the details of Alvina's six months at Islington.' Or again, his intervention in chapter six: 'So far the story of Alvina is commonplace enough. It

[4] *Letters,* pp. 506 ff.

is more or less the story of thousands of girls. . . . And if we were dealing with an ordinary girl we should have to carry on mildly and dully down the long years of employment; or, at the best, marriage with some dull schoolteacher or office-clerk.' It looks as if Lawrence was anxious to get a move-on to the point when he could get Alvina and Cicio away from England, but was held up by the need to provide something reasonably familiar to his reading public. And even in these earlier chapters there are brilliant things, especially those foreshadowing what is coming later. The European-Japanese wrestler, for instance,

> clothed with the most exquisite tattooing. Never would she forget the eagle that flew with terrible spread wings between his shoulders, or the strange mazy pattern that netted the roundness of his buttocks. He was not very large, but nicely shaped, and with no hair on his smooth, tattooed body. . . . A serpent went round his loins and his haunches. . . . He was a queer, black-eyed creature, with a look of silence and toadlike lewdness. . . . A strange sight he was in Woodhouse, on a sunny morning; a snappy-looking bit of riff-raff of the East, rather down at the heel. Who could have imagined the terrible eagle of his shoulders, the serpent of his loins, his supple magic skin? [5]

Already we can see the kind of interest that led Lawrence in the end to *The Plumed Serpent*. And even in England Alvina is beginning to find, in her encounters with Cicio, something of the strange and profound experience that life with him will bring her.

> For a second, she struggled frenziedly. But almost instantly she recognized how much stronger he was, and she was still, mute and motionless with anger. . . . She let herself go down the unknown dark flood of his will, borne from her old footing forever. There comes a moment when fate sweeps us away. Now Alvina felt herself swept—she knew not whither—but into a dusky region where men had dark faces and translucent yellow eyes, where all speech was foreign and life was not her life. It was as if she had fallen from her own

[5] *Lost Girl,* p. 134.

world on to another, darker star, where meanings were all changed.[6]

But it is as we move out of England that the latent life begins really to stir.

All was very still in the wintry sunshine of the Channel. So they turned to walk to the stern of the boat. And Alvina's heart suddenly contracted. . . . For there behind, behind all the sunshine, was England. England, beyond the water, rising with ash-grey, corpse-grey cliffs, and streaks of snow on the downs above. England, like a long, ash-grey coffin slowly submerging. She watched it, fascinated and terrified. It seemed to repudiate the sunshine, to remain unilluminated, long and ash-grey and dead, with streaks of snow like cerements. That was England! Her thoughts flew to Woodhouse, the grey centre of it all. Home! Her heart died within her.[7]

And so we travel to Italy and to Pescocalascio on the edge of the Abruzzi; and here the wonderful descriptive affection in Lawrence, which he had once used for the English countryside (and was not to use for that again until *Lady Chatterley*), reawakens. More than affection: it is as if Lawrence could steal his fingers under the ribs of a country and softly feel its inner movements.

She was only stunned with the strangeness of it all: startled, half-enraptured with the terrific beauty of the place, half-horrified by its savage annihilation of her. . . . It seems there are places which resist us, which have the power to overthrow our psychic being. It seems as if every country had its potent negative centres, localities which savagely and triumphantly refuse our living culture. And Alvina had struck one of these.

Letters from England only wound her—' the world beyond could not help, but it still had the power to injure one here '. Yet still at moments England calls her back—as, for instance, when she contrasts the ' social confidence of England ' with the ' ancient malevolence of the remote,

[6] *ibid.*, p. 256.
[7] *ibid.*, p. 321.

somewhat gloomy hill-peasantry'. And the novel ends a little wistfully, though with a lovely delicate assurance. Cicio is going off to the war, into which Italy has now entered, and Alvina is left behind, in the strange country, and expecting their child; but revived by the knowledge that he will come back to her.

> He sat motionless for a long while: while she undressed and brushed her hair and went to bed. And still he sat there unmoving, like a corpse....
>
> At last he stirred—he rose. He came hesitating across to her.
>
> 'I'll come back, Allaye,' he said quietly. 'Be damned to them all.'
>
> She heard unspeakable pain in his voice.
>
> 'To whom?' she said, sitting up.
>
> He did not answer, but put his arms round her.
>
> 'I'll come back, and we'll go to America,' he said.
>
> 'You'll come back to me,' she whispered, in an ecstasy of pain and relief. It was not her affair, where they should go, so long as he really returned to her.
>
> 'I'll come back,' he said.
>
> 'Sure,' she whispered, straining him to her.

II

Several of Lawrence's short stories contain hints of the same movement, the movement away from, and mourning over, *England, my England*. We need not stay to examine most of them, but there is one, written in 1921 in Sicily, of which Lawrence says he thinks it has 'the quick of a new thing'[8]: *Ladybird*. It is a fascinating little tale, told with liveliness, and contains not a few hints of themes which he will work up at length later on. Lady Daphne's husband, Basil Apsley, is a prisoner of war in Turkey. While he is away his wife visits a hospital for wounded German prisoners, and there gets to know Count Dionys Psanek. Dionys

[8] *Letters*, p. 569.

is recovering from serious wounds, and having been very near death has returned with a strange new existence. Major Apsley returns, but Daphne realizes he is not the same man—both in appearance, because of his scars, and in his inner being. She falls in love with Dionys, but realizes that cannot be permanent—he will go away and she cannot go with him. Yet what they had had together was there, was eternal.

> Two things were struggling in him, the sense of eternal solitude, like space, and the rush of dark flame that would throw him out of his solitude towards her. He was thinking . . . of the future. He had no future in this world: of that he was conscious. . . . Future in the world he could not give her. . . . Why not take the soul she offered him? Now and forever, for the life that would come when they both were dead. Take her into the underworld. Take her into the dark Hades with him, like Francesca and Paolo. . . . 'Listen', he said to her softly. 'Now you are mine. In the dark you are mine. And when you die you are mine. . . . In the day I cannot claim you. . . . I shall have to go away soon. So don't forget—you are the night-wife of the lady-bird' [*sc.* his family seal] 'while you live and even when you die.'

And when he goes, though she is reconciled happily to her husband and loves the family home, she finds that a part of her, the 'dark part', has gone with him.

Aaron's Rod (written in Florence and Baden-Baden, 1921) is, like *The Lost Girl,* the story of a flight from England, from domesticity, from faded conventional values. But this time it is not flight into the arms of a foreign lover; hardly a flight *into* anything; just a flight. It has been very variously assessed. Mr Murry thought it Lawrence's greatest—largely because it has a freshness which *Women in Love* has not. It has moments of great vitality, and the satire on Bloomsbury is lighter, less acid, than that in *Women in Love*. But the English sections are much less successful even than those in *The Lost Girl,* and it is a weakness that one of the main characters, Rawdon Lilly (who is a mouthpiece for Lawrence's own musings), is even more shadowy than his counterpart in *Women in Love,* Rupert Birkin. Still less can we believe in the much more shadowy Tanny, Lilly's Norwegian wife. Moreover the mechanics of the tale rattle badly in places. We find blatant links like 'Our story will not yet see daylight',[9] 'Therefore behold our hero alighting at Novara',[10] or—worst of all—'Don't grumble at me then, gentle reader, and swear at me that this damned fellow wasn't half clever enough to think all these smart things, and realize all these fine-drawn-out subtleties. You are quite right, he wasn't, yet it all resolved itself in him as I say, and it is for you to prove that it didn't.'[11]

Nevertheless there is something very original and very moving about the hero of the novel, Aaron Sisson. His mother 'had wanted Aaron to be a school-teacher. He had served three years' apprenticeship, then suddenly thrown it up and gone to the pit. . . . He had a curious quality of an intelligent, almost sophisticated mind, which had repudiated education. On purpose he kept the Midland accent in his speech. . . . He preferred to be illiterate.' His withdrawal from his wife, his children, his home surroundings, and later his country, is quiet, determined and unemotional, and superbly described. He is having his last look at his home:

> Aaron sat in the open shed at the bottom of his own garden, looking out on the rainy darkness. No one knew he was there. . . . From where he sat, he looked straight up the garden to the house. . . . It was like looking at his home through the wrong end of a telescope. . . Uneasily, he looked along the whole range of houses. The street sloped downhill, and the backs were open to the fields. So he saw a curious succession of lighted windows, between which jutted the intermediary back premises, scullery and outhouse, in dark little blocks. It was something like the key-board of a piano: more still like a succession of musical notes. . . . And thus the whole

[9] *Aaron's Rod,* p. 43.
[10] *ibid.,* p. 139.
[11] *ibid.,* p. 175.

> private life of the street was threaded with lights. There was a sense of indecent exposure, from so many backs.... So many houses cheek by jowl, so many squirming lives, so many back yards, back doors, giving on to the night. It was revolting.

Lilly too, the writer, wants to escape from England, from all that the war has meant there; but his revolt is much more explicit and fully formed. Indeed, the real skill of the book is in the way it shows Aaron and Lilly coming to hold much the same views—of love, of the destiny of the individual, of the meaning of nation and politics—though in such different ways. Aaron is always a little behind, feeling his way inarticulately, often sharply disagreeing with his mentor. Both of them are strongly attached to each other, and yet loose and ready at any minute to come apart—as, indeed, they do from time to time. Their difference can be studied in the scene where a military acquaintance of Lilly's, Herbertson, comes into Lilly's flat, after Aaron's bout of 'flu, and talks ghastly (and very exaggerated) war-talk. Lilly bursts out afterwards:

> I *knew* the war was false: humanly quite false. I always knew it was false. The Germans were false, we were false, everybody was false.... Damn all leagues. Damn all masses and groups, anyhow. All I want is to get *myself* out of their horrible heap.... All that mass-consciousness, all that mass-activity—it's the most horrible nightmare to me.

It is Aaron who intervenes with a common-sense which annoys Lilly and separates them for a time.

As in *The Lost Girl,* it is Italy which first really rouses Lawrence's prose from its semi-slumbers. This has the effect of emphasizing the departure from England; and the same effect is produced by the fact that most of the English people Aaron meets abroad are more or less repulsive. The only exception is Sir William Franks, who, as Horace Gregory points out, is Lawrence's only successful picture of a rich self-made man: and he, set uselessly in the midst of a superb countryside, is significantly afraid of death. By contrast with him, ' Aaron strolled on, surprised himself at his gallant feeling of liberty: a feeling of bravado and almost swaggering carelessness which is Italy's best gift to an Englishman. He had crossed the dividing line, and the values of life, though ostensibly and verbally the same, were dynamically different.'

It is consistent with this development of Aaron's that he lives really in his flute, his ' rod '; and that what he prefers to play is either Scarlatti, or some sixteenth-century Christmas melody—or, better still, ' a bit of medieval phrasing written for the pipe and the viol '. Lawrence was, we are told, not very deeply musical; he had no sense of rhythm for dancing (according to Mabel Dodge Luhan), and though he loved to sing he did not much enjoy his Danish friend's, Knud Merrild's, flute-playing in Mexico.[12] However, he was a friend of Cecil Sharp and of Peter Warlock, and had been introduced to the best of early English music. Aaron plays, and to the Marchesa del Torre (an American married to an Italian Marchese) it sounds thus:

> It was a clear, sharp, lilted run-and-fall of notes, not a tune in any sense of the word, and yet a melody: a bright, quick sound of pure animation. . . . It was like a bird's singing, in that it had no human emotion or passion or intention or meaning—a ripple and poise of animate sound. It made the piano seem a ponderous, nerve-racking steam-roller of noise, and the violin, as we know it, a hateful wire-drawn nerve-torturer.

Finally she is drawn into singing, for the first time for some years:

> She sang free, with the flute gliding along with her. And oh, how beautiful it was for her! . . . How sweet it was to move pure and unhampered at last in the music! The lovely ease and lilt of her own soul in its motion through the music! She wasn't aware of the flute. She didn't know there was anything

[12] Knud Merrild, *A Poet and Two Painters*, p. 133.

> except her own pure lovely song-drift. Her soul seemed to breathe as a butterfly breathes, as it rests on a leaf and slowly breathes its wings.

This awakens desire in Aaron. For such a long time

> he had been gripped inside himself, and withheld. . . . All his deep, desirous blood had been locked, he had wanted nobody, and nothing. . . . And now came his desire back. But strong, fierce as iron. . . . Aaron's black rod of power, blossoming again with red Florentine lilies and fierce thorns.

Actually his love-affair with the Marchesa turns out a failure in the end: this is the complement to the later smashing of his flute. But having once budded, it will bud again. Lilly told him, 'It's a reed, a water-plant. You can't kill it.'

III

Although the English characters in *Aaron's Rod* do not come out very well, except for Aaron himself and Lilly (Tanny, we remember, is Norwegian; and Lilly himself seems quite raceless): yet it is significant that there are no Italian characters that come out any better. Lawrence, in fact, has moved a stage beyond the point reached in *The Lost Girl.* Contrasting England and Italy, he has to admit of the latter that

> Alas, however, the verbal and the ostensible, the accursed mechanical ideal gains day by day over the spontaneous life-dynamic, so that Italy becomes as idea-bound and as automatic as England: just a business proposition.[13]

And we are beginning to see that what started as an escape from England will have to turn into a flight from Europe. Aaron was so impressed at first with the newness and strangeness of Italy that he had 'no eye for the horrible sameness that was spreading like a disease over Italy from

[13] *Aaron's Rod,* p. 162.

England and the north. . . . Alas, the one world triumphing more and more over the many worlds, the big oneness swallowing up the many small diversities in its insatiable gnawing appetite, leaving a dreary sameness throughout the world, that means at last complete sterility.'[14] Lilly had planned to go to Malta and Italy, but at the back of his mind he wanted to range further. Lilly had sat in London reading Frobenius (this gives us the source of Lawrence's thoughts about Africa in *Women in Love*), and muses about 'Old, old dark Africa, and the world before the flood'. But it is with stranger prescience that he thinks:

> I would have loved the Aztecs and the Red Indians. I *know* they hold the elements in life which I am looking for—they had living pride. Not like the flea-bitten Asiatics. . . . The American races—and the South Sea Islanders—the Marquesans, the Maori blood. That was the true blood. It wasn't frightened.

For it is ultimately Mexico that has the strongest pull on him, and, as we shall see, that left its deepest mark on him too. At any rate here we see clearly forming the determination of Lawrence to explore older lands and older cultures, for, like Lilly, 'his soul had the faculty of divesting itself of the moment, and seeking further, deeper interests'. A little later (1921) when on a visit to Sardinia he saw the same problem beginning to face the people there as already faced Italy:

> Their life is centripetal, pivoted inside itself, and does not run out towards others and mankind. One feels for the first time the real old medieval life, which is enclosed in itself and has no interest in the world outside. . . . It is wonderful in them that at this time of day they still wear the long stocking-caps as part of their inevitable selves. It is a sign of obstinate and powerful tenacity. They are not going to be broken in upon by world-consciousness. They are not going into the world's common clothes. . . . And one cannot help wondering whether Sardinia will resist right through. Will the last waves

[14] *ibid.*, p. 163.

> of enlightenment and world-unity break over them and wash away the stocking-caps? [15]

And then Lawrence goes on, with that unusual prophetic insight which he sometimes had and to which we shall have to refer again:

> Certainly a reaction is setting in, away from the old universality, back, away from cosmopolitanism and internationalism. Russia, with her Third International, is at the same time reacting most violently away from all other contact, back, recoiling on herself, into a fierce, unapproachable Russianism. Which motion will conquer? The workman's International, or the centripetal movement into national isolation? Are we going to merge into one grey proletarian homogeneity?—or are we going to swing back into more or less isolated, separate, defiant communities?
>
> Probably both. The workman's International movement will finally break the flow towards cosmopolitanism and world-assimilation, and suddenly in a crash the world will fly back into intense separations....
>
> For myself I ... shall be glad when men fiercely react against looking all alike, and being all alike, and betake themselves into vivid clan or nation-distinctions.

IV

Lawrence was, in fact, what we should now call a 'regionalist', and it was that more than anything which drove him into isolation from his countrymen and their politics. He has been claimed by Marxist critics as having been on the side of 'the workers'; and by others as a forerunner of fascism. There is a *prima facie* case for the latter claim, as we shall see especially when we come to *The Plumed Serpent;* but not a case that will bear very close examination. As to the Marxists' claim, it would be truer to say that he foresaw the effects of communism upon small agricultural

[15] *Sea and Sardinia* (1923), p. 134.

nations, of which recent events in Jugoslavia have been so symbolic. From his earliest contacts with the Fabian world he seems to have rejected socialism. In his first novel, *The White Peacock,* we find George and Lettie arguing. George had gone in for open-air harangues in defence of labour, and Lettie says:

> Of course I have read Mr Wells and Mr Shaw, and even Neil Lyons and a Dutchman—what is his name, Querido? But what can I do? I think the rich have as much misery as the poor, and of quite as deadly a sort. . . .

And later she writes to Cyril about George's politics:

> Of course, I am in sympathy with the socialists, but I cannot narrow my eyes till I see one thing only. . . . The people are so earnest, they make me sad. But then, they are so didactic they hold forth so much, they are so cocksure and so narrow-eyed, they make me laugh.[16]

And George himself soon tires of the movement. A characteristic remark of Lawrence's occurs in one of the Memoirs; hearing about a young woman of his acquaintance, who has been violently converted to left-wing politics, he observes sadly: ' I'm sorry she has lost her religion.'

Yet Lawrence never lost his sympathy for the working men and especially for the miners. If we find him, for instance in the play *Touch and Go*, unduly scornful of their political selves, he is certainly no whit more respectful to the owners. In *The Rainbow* Ursula goes to stay with her uncle, Tom Brangwen, who is a manager by now. Lawrence's picture of the pit village, Wiggiston, is unforgettable. On a hill outside stands Tom's house. Ursula and he argue about the conditions.

> ' They seem unutterably, unutterably sad,' said Ursula, out of a passionate throat.
>
> ' I don't think they are that. They just take it for granted.'
>
> ' What do they take for granted? '
>
> ' This—the pits and the place altogether.'

[16] *The White Peacock,* pp. 450 ff.

'Why don't they alter it?' she passionately protested.
'They believe they must alter themselves to fit the pits and the place, rather than alter the pits and the place to fit themselves. It is easier,' he said.

A servant comes in to ask about the tea, and later Ursula asks about her. Tom replies:

> She is a widow. Her husband died of consumption a little while ago. . . . He lay there in the house-place at their mother's, and five or six other people in the house, and died very gradually. I asked her if his death wasn't a great trouble to her. 'Well,' she said, 'he was fretful towards the last, never satisfied, never easy, always fret-fretting, an' never knowing what would satisfy him. So in one way it was a relief when it was over—for him and for everybody. . . . You see, you get used to it. I've had my father and two brothers go off just the same. You get used to it.'

And Tom then comments on the miners' lives and morals:

> Marriage and home is a little side-show. The women know it right enough, and take it for what it's worth. One man or another, it doesn't matter all the world. The pit matters. Round the pit there will always be the side-shows, plenty of 'em. . . . They're not interested enough to be very immoral—it all amounts to the same thing, moral or immoral—just a question of pit wages. The most moral duke in England makes two hundred thousand a year out of these pits. He keeps the morality end up.[17]

In *Women in Love* we find the contrast between the new and the old mining policy expressed in the contrast between Gerald Crich and his father. The old man, Thomas Crich, nearly broke his heart because of a strike: for he was 'trapped between two half-truths, and broken. He wanted to be a pure Christian, one and equal with all men. He even wanted to give away all he had, to the poor. Yet he was a great promoter of industry.' Gerald has no such sentimentalities: he 'abandoned the whole democratic-equality problem as a piece of silliness. What mattered was

[17] *The Rainbow*, pp. 328 ff.

the great social productive machine.' So he sets out to reorganize the whole system. At first the men resist the innovations; but gradually they submit to it all.

> The joy went out of their lives, the hope seemed to perish as they became more and more mechanized. And yet they accepted the new conditions. They even got a further satisfaction out of them. . . . There was a new world, a new order, strict, terrible, inhuman, but satisfying in its very destructiveness. The men were satisfied to belong to the great and wonderful machine, even whilst it destroyed them. . . . It was the first great phase of chaos, the substitution of the mechanical principle for the organic, the destruction of the organic purpose, the organic unity. . . .

We shall see Lawrence returning indirectly to this theme in *Lady Chatterley*. And in the very last year of his life he looked back and wrote an article which confirms what he had said in 1915 about the contrast between new and old mining:

> The life was a curious cross between industrialism and the old agricultural England of Shakespeare and Milton and Fielding and George Eliot. . . . The people lived almost entirely by instinct, men of my father's age could not really read. And the pit did not mechanize men. On the contrary. Under the butty system, the miners worked underground as a sort of intimate community. . . . My father loved the pit. . . . The great fallacy is, to pity the man. . . . He was happy: or more than happy, he was fulfilled. . . . But in my generation, the boys I went to school with, colliers now, have all been beaten down, what with the din-din-dinning of Board Schools, books, cinemas, clergymen, the whole nation and human consciousness hammering on the fact of material prosperity above all things. . . . Even the farm-labourer to-day is psychologically a town-bird.[18]

Given this fundamental contrast, between a mechanistic and an organic approach to social and industrial problems, it can easily be seen why Lawrence rejected the usual political solutions of his day.

[18] Nottingham and the Mining Countryside, *New Adelphi*, August, 1930: *Phoenix*, pp. 135 ff.

> The Conservative talks about the old and glorious national ideal, the Liberal talks about this great struggle for right in which the nation is engaged, the peaceful women talk about disarmament and international peace. Bertie Russell talks about democratic control and the educating of the artisan, and all this, all this goodness, is just a warm and cosy cloak for a bad spirit. They all want the same thing: a continuing in this state of disintegration wherein each separate little ego is an independent little principality by itself.[19]

All this might lead to a romantic kind of anti-mechanism, to vague cries of ' Smash the machine '. But Lawrence is too level-headed for this.

> The inventor of the labour-saving machine has been hailed as a public benefactor, and we have rejoiced over his discovery. Now there is a railing against the machine, as if it were an evil thing. And the thinkers talk about the return to the medieval system of handicrafts. Which is absurd.
>
> As I look round this room, at the bed, at the counterpane, at the books and chairs and the little bottles, and think that machines made them, I am glad. I am very glad of the bedstead, of the white enamelled iron with brass rail. . . . Its lines are straight and parallel, or at right angles, giving a sense of static motionlessness. . . . There is nothing there to hurt me or to hinder me; my wish for something to serve my purpose is perfectly fulfilled.
>
> Which is what a machine can do. It can provide me with the perfect mechanical instrument, a thing mathematically and scientifically correct. . . . But to what pitiable misuse is it put! . . . Why, when man, in his godly effort, has produced a means to freedom, do we make it a means to more slavery? [20]

Indeed, Lawrence has some fun with ' smashers ' of all kinds. It is significant that *Aaron's Rod* begins with rather vapid conversations in which the bright young intellectuals show off their ' Bolshie ' sympathies. ' Wouldn't I love it,' cries Josephine, ' if they'd make a bloody revolution.' But

[19] *Letters* (1915), p. 247.
[20] *Study of Hardy* (*Phoenix,* p. 426).

the novel ends with a bit of actual violence—the bomb-throwing which destroys Aaron's 'rod', his flute. 'Here was a blow he had not expected. And the loss was for him symbolistic. It chimed with something in his soul: the bomb, the smashed flute, the end.' Here, too, in political violence, Lawrence is saying, lies a kind of death.

It is interesting, however, that the bomb was thrown by an anarchist. For Lawrence had sympathy with anarchism, and was evidently in two minds about it even as a possible political way. This is revealed in a curious and arresting passage in *Twilight in Italy,* to which very little attention has been paid by the critics. He meets a little group of Italians, exiled in Switzerland, and all anarchists. (As the passage is not well known, I give it fairly fully.)

> They loved Italy passionately; but they would not go back. All their blood, all their sense were Italian, needed the Italian sky, the speech, the sensuous life. . . . Yet a new tiny flower was struggling to open in them, the flower of a new spirit. . . .
>
> '*Sa signore*' (one of them says), '*L'uomo non ha patria*—a man has no country. What has the Italian Government to do with us? What does a Government mean? It makes us work, it takes a part of our wages away from us, it makes us soldiers—and what for?'

Lawrence then discovers that they themselves had evaded military service, and that was why they could not go back, had forfeited parents as well as homeland.

> 'What does the Government do?' the Italian goes on. 'It takes taxes; it has an army and police, and it makes roads. But we could do without an army, and we could be our own police, and we could make our own roads.'

Lawrence does not condemn them, and is extremely embarrassed.

> I did not want to answer. I could feel a new spirit in him, something strange and pure and slightly frightening. He wanted something which was beyond me. And my soul was

> somewhere in tears, crying helplessly like an infant in the night. . . . He seemed to look at me, me, an Englishman, an educated man, for corroboration. But I could not corroborate him. I knew the purity and new struggling towards birth of a true star-like spirit. But I could not confirm him in his utterance. . . . I did not believe in the perfectibility of man. I did not believe in infinite harmony among men. And this was his star, this belief.

They gave him a little anarchist paper of theirs, but he did not read it, and the next morning slipped away early so as to miss them.

> I did not want to see the Italians. Something had got tied up in me, and I could not bear to see them again. I liked them so much; but for some reason or other, my mind stopped like clockwork if I wanted to think of them and of what their lives would be, their future. . . . I could never write to them, or think of them, or even read the paper they gave me. . . . The moment my memory touched them, my whole soul stopped and was null.

Here Lawrence wonderfully expresses his own feelings and attitude. But the reason for that embarrassment is surely perfectly clear. Here was a group of men whose experience and reaction had been very similar to his, but whose resultant policy and methods he could not wholly endorse. They were at once so right and so wrong; and to applaud or to condemn them would equally be to commit himself in ways he could not at that moment be committed.

V

In his next novel, *Kangaroo* (commenced in Australia in the summer of 1922 and finished in Taos, New Mexico, that autumn), the political discussion becomes quite explicit. So explicit, indeed, that many critics have dismissed the novel as of no value, except for its long parenthetical chapter containing the scarcely-veiled autobiography of his war-time experience in Cornwall. But there is much more in it than that. For here, perhaps more clearly than anywhere else, we find Lawrence's astonishing capacity for not merely sensing the atmosphere but digging out the whole 'psychic history' of a country in a few weeks' visit. After a little more than a month there he was writing to Mrs Carswell:

> It *is* a weird place. In the *established* sense, it is socially nil. Happy-go-lucky, don't-you-bother, we're-in-Australia. But also there seems to be no inside life of any sort: just a long lapse and drift.... [Yet] the country has an extraordinary hoary, weird attraction. As you get used to it, it seems so *old*, as if it had missed all this Semite-Egyptian-Indo-European vast era of history, and was coal age, the age of great ferns and mosses. It hasn't got a consciousness—just none—too far back....[21]

And then here is the strange new society, jumped up in a night, moving on the face of the old, old country. By contrast with that, he rediscovers the aristocratic principle of Europe.

> Europe is really established upon the aristocratic principle. Remove the sense of class distinction, of higher and lower, and you have anarchy in Europe. But in Australia, it seemed to Somers, the distinction was already gone.... In Australia nobody is supposed to rule, and nobody does rule.... And this was what Somers could not stand.... The working classes in England feel just the same about it as do the upper classes.... Somers was a true Englishman, with an Englishman's hatred of anarchy.... So he felt himself at a discount in Australia.

And the consciousness of the people is, Lawrence finds, affected by this: it makes them live purely at the top of their minds and senses. Take Jack Calcott:

> Somers tolerated with difficulty Jack's facetious familiarity and heartiness.... The same breezy intimacy with all of them, and the moment they had passed by, they didn't exist

21 *Letters* (1922), p. 549.

> for him any more than the gull that had curved across the air. . . . Like so many Flying Dutchmen the Australian's acquaintances seemed to steer slap through his consciousness, and were gone on the wind. . . . Somers felt that if he knew Jack for twenty years, and then went away, Jack would say: 'Friend o' mine, Englishman, rum sort of bloke, not a bad sort. Dunno where he's hanging out just now. Somewhere on the surface of the old humming-top, I suppose.'[22]

As Somers observes significantly to Jack later, 'somebody will have to water Australia with their blood before it's a real country. The soil, the very plants seem to be waiting for it.'

Significantly, because Australia gets watered with blood before the end of the book—with Kangaroo's blood. But it does not seem to bring fertility, unless we see signs of a real native budding in the second Australian novel, *Boy in the Bush,* and that is only partly of Lawrence's authorship. *Kangaroo* leaves us chiefly with a sense of wide, open barrenness: the wonderful description of the little house by the coast, 'Coo-ee', seems to tell us that it is the sea—the surf and the eternal relentless breakers—that is really alive.

And as for the political theme, Lawrence's rejection of Kangaroo's fascism seems quite decisive. Kangaroo himself, the fat little violent, affectionate, shouting Jewish autocrat, is very sympathetically portrayed, and when he dies Somers is deeply affected. And yet Somers rejects his programme, and will not attend his funeral. On the other side is the socialist, Willie Struthers. Critics who are anxious to make out a fascist pedigree for Lawrence emphasize his devastating analysis of Struthers' programme. Mr Eric Bentley, for instance, says that 'The communist leader [*sic*], Willie Struthers, is represented as lean and covetous. He embodies mere *lust* for power . . .' and that the motive of Communism is described as 'envy and the denial of authority'.[23] This

[22] *Kangaroo,* p. 60.
[23] Eric Bentley, *Cult of the Superman,* p. 214.

seems to me quite unfair. Lawrence does his best to give Struthers a good chance to express his views, and shows Struthers intelligent enough to appreciate Somers' objections. Somers has just expressed doubt as to whether Labour will ever really rise to act:

> Struthers did not seem to hear this. At least he did not answer. He sat with his head dropped, fingering the blotter, rather like a boy who is being told things he hates to hear but which he doesn't deny.
>
> At last he looked up, and the fighting look was in the front of his eyes.
>
> 'It may be as you say, Mr Somers,' he replied. 'Men may not be ready yet for any great change. That does not make the change less inevitable. It's coming, and it's got to come.'[24]

And at the end of Struthers' exposition—by no means a caricature—of the Labour case, Somers is moved in spite of himself.

> A strange glow had come into his [Struthers'] large black eyes, something glistening and half-sweet, fixing itself on you. You felt drawn towards a strange sweetness—perhaps poisonous. Yet it touched Richard [Somers] on one of his quivering strings—the latent power that is in man today, to love his near mate with a passionate, absolutely trusting love. . . .

And yet he knows the dangers of this kind of 'absolute love'. After all, he himself

> did love the working people, he did know them capable of a great, generous love for one another. And he did also believe, in a way, that they were capable of building up this great Church of Christ, the great beauty of a People, upon the generous passion of mate-love. All this theoretical socialism started by Jews like Marx, and appealing only to the will-to-power in the masses, making money the whole crux, this has cruelly injured the working people of Europe.

[24] *Kangaroo,* p. 219.

And he sees that the Struthers way will not bring about what is needed. And so comes his real answer to the problem left by the rejection of both solutions, Kangaroo's and Struthers': the answer he has been feeling for throughout his novels up to this point but now at last clearly formulates and finds a name for. (Having refused the false absolutes):

> Yet the human heart must have an absolute. It is one of the conditions of being human. The only thing is the God who is the source of all passion. Once go down before the God-passion and human passions take their right rhythm.... With no deep God who is source of all passion and life to hold them separate and yet sustained in accord, the loving comrades would smash one another.... Any more love is a hopeless thing, till we have found again... the great dark God who alone will sustain us in our loving one another.

But having announced his religious answer, Somers withdraws from the struggle. It is significant that in the end the only Australian he really respects is 'Jaz' (William James Trewhella, a coal and wood merchant) who seems to have a foot in both political camps, and is a Cornishman with a Cornish accent still audible beneath his Australian twang. The withdrawal hurts Somers—'They are my fellow-men, they are my fellow-men', he murmurs helplessly—but he can't be on either side. And when he learns that Kangaroo is definitely dying he flies from Sydney to the sea to be by himself:

> Immediately the great rhythm and ringing of the breakers obliterated every other feeling in his breast, and his soul was a moonlit hollow with the waves striding home.

There follows a passage describing Somers' desolation which seems to me one of the finest Lawrence ever wrote. It has been suggested by Mr Walter Allen[25] that Lawrence was 'a mystic of a sort'. If the word is used in a very loose

[25] Walter Allen, 'Lawrence in Perspective', *Penguin New Writing*, No. 29 (1947).

sense, for anyone who relies upon intuitive rather than *discursive* knowledge, this may be allowed. In that case it might be said, in an analogical sense, that this passage at the end of chapter seventeen is Lawrence's account of the dark night of the senses. Consider it in that light:

> Richard had it all to himself—the ever-unfurling water, the ragged, flat, square-holed rocks, the fawn sands inland, the soft sand-bank, the sere flat grass where ponies wandered. ... And there ... he drifted into indifference. The far-off, far-off, far-off indifference. The world revolved and revolved and disappeared. Like a stone that has fallen into the sea, his old life, the old meaning, fell, and rippled, and there was vacancy, with the sea and the Australian shore in it. Far-off, far-off, as if he had landed on to another planet, as a man might land after death. Leaving behind the body of care. . . .
>
> To be alone, mindless and memoryless between the sea, under the sombre wall-front of Australia. . . . The strange falling-away of everything. The cabbage palms in the sea-wind were sere like old mops. The jetty straddled motionless from the shore. A pony walked on the sand snuffing the sea-weed. . . .
>
> Old dust and dirt of corpses: words and feelings. The decomposed body of the past whirling and choking us, language, love and meaning. When a man loses his soul he knows what a small, weary bit of clock-work it was. . . . Perhaps it is only the great pause between carings. But it is only in this pause ... that one finds the meaninglessness of meanings, and the other dimension, the reality of timelessness and nowhere.

I think that this, incidentally, gives a clue to the puzzle of the famous autobiographical chapter. Is it just padding (which is what, I fear we must say of chapter fourteen, 'Bits')? Why is it inserted here; is it merely dragged in, with very small justification in the story, to fill out what would be a shortish novel without it? The answer is that it does as a matter of fact illuminate the background of Somers' thought, and elucidate the development of his attitude to the political drama. Somers in a vacuum, without his past history, would be very unaccountable—as Lilly, in

Aaron's Rod, sometimes seems to be for that very reason. And we shall see that Kate in *The Plumed Serpent*, who is thrown at the reader somewhat Melchizedek-like, without a pre-history, is a much more negative character, to whom things happen but who does not mould them. In this novel we are properly prepared for Somers' restlessness. When he arrived in Australia he immediately felt a homesickness for England: ' He felt a long navel string fastening him to Europe, and he wanted to go back, to go home.' It was not, however, to Europe that he went at the end of the novel, but further down into the depths, below the surface levels at which political solutions had failed: to America, to New Mexico and to Old. He and Harriet sailed away ' over a cold, dark, inhospitable sea '. But we know now that at least he has gained a flexibility—achieved through struggle and disappointment—which is itself a positive conquest.

> After all his terrific upheaval, Richard Lovat [Somers] at last gave it up, and went to sleep. A man must even know how to give up his own earnestness, when its hour is over, and not to bother about anything any more.

He is not, after all, the enemy of civilization, as his critics complained: ' I'm the enemy of this machine-civilization and this ideal civilization. But I'm not the enemy of the deep, self-responsible consciousness in man, which is what *I* mean by civilization.' And he is still a lover of his old country, just in the sense that Birkin expressed it some years earlier in *Women in Love*. Birkin and Ursula had found a lovely second-hand armchair in the market, simple, of birch wood:

> ' So beautiful, so pure! ' Birkin said. ' It almost breaks my heart. . . . My beloved country—it had something to express even when it made that chair.'
>
> ' And hasn't it now? ' asked Ursula. She was always angry when he took this tone.
>
> ' No, it hasn't. When I see that clear, beautiful chair, and I think of England, even Jane Austen's England—it had

living thoughts to unfold even then, and pure happiness in unfolding them. And now, we can only fish among the rubbish heaps for the remnants of their old expression. There is no production in us now, only sordid and foul mechanicalness.'

So in *Kangaroo* Somers turns away, and turns back, back:

to the old dark gods, who had waited so long in the outer dark. . . . There is this ever-present, living darkness inexhaustible and unknowable. It *is*. And it is all the God and the gods.

CHAPTER FOUR

THE DEATH OF THE GODS

LAWRENCE's little history book, *Movements in European History* (1921), written a little before *The Lost Girl* (1919), ends with the following paragraphs—which again I quote in full, since the book is little known today:

> So the cycle of European history completes itself, phase by phase, from imperial Rome, through the medieval empire and papacy to the kings of the Renaissance period, on to the great commercial nations, the government by the industrial and commercial middle classes, and so to that last rule, that last oneness, of the labouring people. So Europe moves from oneness to oneness, from the imperial unity to the unity of the labouring classes, from the beginning to the end.
>
> But we must never forget that mankind lives by a twofold motive: the motive of peace and increase, and the motive of contest and martial triumph. As soon as the appetite for martial adventure and triumph in conflict is satisfied, the appetite for peace and increase manifests itself, and vice versa. It seems a law of life. Therefore a great united Europe of productive working-people, all materially equal, will never be able to continue and remain firm unless it unites also round one great chosen figure, some hero who can lead a great war, as well as administer a wide peace. It all depends on the will of the people. But the will of the people must concentrate in one figure, who is also supreme over the will of the people. He must be chosen, but at the same time responsible to God alone. Here is a problem of which a stormy future will have to evolve the solution.[1]

[1] It is significant, too, that the chapter on *The Germans* (cap. iv) is the most arresting in the book.

In *Aaron's Rod,* and above all in *The Ladybird* (1921) there is much talk about the need of a Leader. Count Dionys even pictures the masses coming to such leaders and saying, 'You are greater than we. Be our lords. Take our life and our death in your hands'; and pictures the leader himself replying, 'If you choose me, you give up for ever your right to judge me. . . . You have performed the sacred act of choice. Henceforth you can only obey.' But then we remember that Dionys is a German, and both Basil and Daphne criticize him for his authoritarian ideas. It is evident that Lawrence is not really happy about these views. He puts them much more guardedly into Lilly's mouth; and then finally in the death of the fascist leader in *Kangaroo* we see the death of the *Führer-prinzip.*

How, then, does *Kangaroo* come to be followed (for *The Boy in the Bush* is not Lawrence's designing altogether) by the most 'fascist' novel of all, *The Plumed Serpent* (1926)? It does not look from this as if Lawrence has shaken off the Leader-principle. What else are Ramón and Cipriano really but the equivalent of Brownshirts? Indeed, Cipriano explicitly states a principle which brings unpleasantly familiar echoes to the mind. After the attempt on Don Ramón's life, the four would-be assassins are brought in before the people. Cipriano accuses them:

> 'When many men come against one, what is the name of the many?'
>
> 'Cowards, my Lord,' (reply the Guards).
>
> 'Cowards it is. They are less than men. Men that are less than men are not good enough for the light of the sun. If men that are men will live, men that are less than men must be put away, *lest they multiply too much. . . .*[2] Shall they die?'
>
> 'They shall surely die, my Lord.'

[2] Italics mine.

And so Cipriano stabs each of them, solemnly, before the people. Our minds go back too, perhaps, to Lawrence's defence of flogging in his essay on Dana in *Studies in Classical American Literature.*

But we must pause before making the obvious deduction. For we find him back in 1922, when he was writing *Fantasia of the Unconscious,* already beginning to see the real drift of things. There he shows that there are two directions we may go in, both of them wrong. Forwards to the Brave new World,

> Towards the great terminus where bottles of sterilized milk for the babies are delivered at the bedroom windows by noiseless aeroplanes each morning . . . where nobody ever has to do anything except turn a handle now and then in a spirit of universal love.

Or backwards towards nationalism of a stultifying sort, hankered after by the Germans who cry:

> Reverse engines, and away, away to our city, where the sterilized milk is delivered by noiseless aeroplanes, *at the very precise minute when our great doctors of the Fatherland have diagnosed that it is good for you*: where . . . the friction of eating stimulates the cells of the jawbone and develops the *superman strength of will which makes us gods.*

We have already quoted above his keen foresight into the development of Russian nationalism—the passage from *Sea and Sardinia* given on page 74. Better known is his *Letter from Germany,* written in 1924, and published in the *New Statesman and Nation,* October 13, 1934.[3] As this is fairly easily available, I give only the gist of it here.

> The moment you are in Germany, you know. It feels empty, and, somehow, menacing. . . . The hope in peace-and-production is broken. The old flow, the old adherence is ruptured. And a still older flow has set in. Back, back to the savage polarity of Tartary, and away from the polarity of civilized Christian Europe. . . . These queer gangs of *Young Socialists,*

[3] *Phoenix,* pp. 107 ff.

youths and girls, with their non-materialistic profession, their half-mystic assertions, they strike one as strange. Something primitive, like loose, roving gangs of broken scattered tribes, so they affect one. . . . At the same time, we have brought it about ourselves—by a Ruhr occupation, by an English nullity, and by a German false will.

Later on, after he has returned to Germany in 1926 and seen still more of the Youth movements, his prognostication is confirmed. He writes in 1927:

> I don't believe you'll ever get modern Germans free from an acute sense of their nationality—and in contact with foreigners they'll feel political for years to come. They have no self-possession—and they have that naïve feeling that it's somebody else's fault.[4]

And again, early in 1928:

> Even the German *Bunde,* I am afraid, will drift into nationalistic, and ultimately, fighting bodies: a new, and necessary form of militarism.[5]

What, in the light of all this, are we to think of *The Plumed Serpent?* The answer must be, either that Lawrence has had an almost unbelievable lapse from sanity; or that the theme of this is not, as might appear at first sight, primarily ' political ' at all. That the latter alternative is correct should be clear from the structure of the novel itself. There is, of course, some mention of political rivals—the Mexican socialists, the capitalists; with the, by now, familiar rejection of both—' Bolshevism is one sort of bullying, capitalism another: and liberty is a change of chains '. But it is clear that the dramatic centre of the novel is in chapter seventeen, where Ramón visits the Bishop. And what Ramón provides is more than a popular unifying political movement. He is out explicitly, of course, to revive the old gods; he becomes Quetzalcoatl reincarnate; the central force of his new-old religion lies in the Church—now stripped of

[4] *Letters,* p. 684.
[5] *ibid.,* p. 698.

its Catholic essentials; and he presents the people with a liturgy, hymns, ceremonial, vestments, and even 'day-hours' —marked now, not by bells ringing the Angelus, but by drums sounding at dawn, nine, twelve, three and sunset. (Lawrence, remember, had stayed at a Benedictine monastery with Magnus.[6]) Is it evil, Kate wonders, this 'conscious reverting to the savage'? And she answers herself:

> No! It's not a helpless, panic reversal. It is conscious, carefully chosen. We must go back to pick up old threads. We must take up the old, broken impulse that will connect us with the mystery of the cosmos again, now we are at the end of our tether.

But what has happened? 'Conscious, carefully chosen'? These are the words that by now we have learned to consider as abusive epithets in Lawrence's mouth! And here I believe lies the real weakness of this particular novel—and of one aspect of Lawrence's own philosophy. Most critics have considered *The Plumed Serpent* Lawrence's worst novel—'a grotesque mixture of Rider Haggard's *She* and *Also Sprach Zarathustra*' said the late Mr Hugh Kingsmill.[7] Mrs Carswell alone loyally stands up for it as his greatest—largely because Lawrence himself thought it so soon after he had written it, just as earlier he had considered *Women in Love* his greatest. For myself, I consider it his *greatest* failure. 'Greatest' advisedly, since in some ways his powers are at their strongest in it. In his topographical descriptions, for instance; in the brilliant and ugly realism of the bull-fight; in the extraordinary feat of 'tough', 'thriller' writing when he comes to the attack on Jamiltepec (chapter nineteen); and above all in the ability to convey the constantly threatening elements in life—the threat of rain, of the drums, of silence, of mass hypnosis. If anybody could have brought it off, Lawrence could. But in fact nobody could. The creation of a new religion, fully-fledged, in a setting where twentieth-century Americans and Irish mix

[6] M. Magnus, Introduction to *Memoirs of the Foreign Legion*.
[7] H. Kingsmill, *Life of D. H. Lawrence,* Methuen, 1938, p. 216.

with primitive Mexicans, was an impossible task. There are places which show the same kind of technical weakness that we detected in *Aaron's Rod.* (The passage, for instance, when he breaks out, in his most vapid journalese: 'Oh America, with your unspeakable hard lack of charm, what then is your final meaning! . . . Charmless America! With your hard, vindictive beauty, are you waiting forever to smite death? . . .' etc.) Moreover, we occasionally have the sense that Lawrence is not quite happy about it all. Kate is 'shocked and depressed' at the execution of prisoners mentioned above: 'Deep in her soul came a revulsion against this manifestation of pure will'. In the end she does submit, but it is a submission, and is only worth it, apparently, because the alternative—to become a 'grey grimalkin' of fifty-five in a London drawing-room—is too unpleasant. 'You won't let me go', she says to Cipriano; and these are the closing words of the novel.

It is dangerous to bring the 'personal element' into criticism. But it is perhaps worth observing that the weaknesses which could have been detected by purely literary criticism are confirmed by the knowledge that at this time Lawrence was uneasy about Frieda. She was home-sick for her children, and she went on ahead back to Europe, while he stayed on for a time in Mexico, hoping to follow her later; and those who knew them have hinted that Lawrence was not sure that he and Frieda would meet again. Moreover, if the account given by the two Danish painters, Götzsche and Merrild, is reliable, Lawrence was often in an exceptionally nervy state in New Mexico and after. Some have gone so far as to use the word 'paranoiac'. Even if that is an exaggeration, it certainly seems that his ungovernable temper was more than usually evident. What is certain is that Lawrence revised his view of *The Plumed Serpent* later. In 1925 he had called the latter his 'most important novel so far'.[8] But *Lady Chatterley* soon absorbed him

[8] *Letters,* p. 637.

more. And in 1928 we find him writing to Wytter Bynner: 'I sniffed the red herring in your last letter a long time: then at last decided it's a live sprat. I mean about *The Plumed Serpent* and "the hero". On the whole, I think you're right. The hero is obsolete, and the leader of men is a back number. After all, at the back of the hero is the militant ideal: and the militant ideal . . . seems to me also a cold egg. . . . The new relationship will be some sort of tenderness, sensitive, between men and men and men and women.' [9] 'Tenderness' leads straight, of course, to *Lady Chatterley*.

But before we come to that we must notice another factor which explains the transition from *The Plumed Serpent* to *Lady Chatterley*. In the 'D. H. Lawrence Number' of *The Laughing Horse* (April, 1926) [10] Lawrence wrote an article on 'Europe *v*. America', which is very self-revealing. It is here that he says, 'As for Europe's being old, I find it much younger than America' (he said the same, we remember, of Australia). And he goes on, very frankly,

> I've been a fool myself, saying: Europe is finished for me. It wasn't Europe at all, it was myself, keeping a strangle-hold on myself. And that strangle-hold I carried over to America; as many a man—and woman, worse still—has done before me. Now, back in Europe, I feel a real relief. . . . Europe is squeezing the life out of herself, with her mental education and fixed ideas. But she hasn't got her hands round her own throat not half so far as America has hers.

When first he got to New Mexico, he wrote from Taos:

> Perhaps it is necessary for me to try these places, perhaps it is my destiny to know the world. It only excites the outside of me. The inside it leaves more isolated and stoic than ever. . . . It is all a form of running away from oneself and the great problems: all this wild west and the strange Australia. But I try to keep quite clear.[11]

[9] *ibid.*, p. 711.
[10] *Phoenix*, pp. 117 ff.
[11] *Letters* (1922), p. 556.

And he constantly wavered, when in Mexico, whether to stay or to return to Europe. Mabel Dodge Luhan, his American friend, wife of an Indian, who originally lured him out to New Mexico, observed that Mexico mattered to Lawrence more than New Mexico, in spite of the fact that his scenes supposed to be set in Mexico are full of experience he has picked up among the New Mexican Indians. And she suggests that the reason why Mexico mattered more to him was that 'Mexico has some written "history"; New Mexico has none', and that this is a sign that Lawrence never really escaped from his past or the past of his race, never got outside the 'meaningless human somersaults' which is all history consists of.[12] This, which is meant to be damning, is an interesting point in Lawrence's favour: his profound sense of the past reasserts itself. But his hesitations about the present are there none the less. Before he left New Mexico, in 1925, he wrote his Biblical play, *David,* which is not so well-known as it deserves. And there is little doubt that he, David Herbert, has put something of his experience of this period into the hero of it.

> SAMUEL: It is time thou shouldst go. As a fox with the dogs upon him, hast thou much fleeing to do.
> DAVID: Must I always flee, my Father? I am already weary of flight.
> SAMUEL: Yea, to flee away is thy portion. . . . Flee thou, flee, and flee again, and once more, flee. So shalt thou at last have the kingdom and the glory in the sight of men.

The best writing in the play comes in the 'prophesyings' of Saul, which foretell the death of the gods:

> Yea, and I see death, death, death! And the seed of David rising up and covering the earth. . . . And they thicken and thicken, till the world's air grates and clicks as with the wings of locusts. And man is his own devourer, and the Deep turns away, without wish to look on him further. So the earth is desert, and manless, yet covered with houses and iron. Yea, David, the pits are digged even under the feet of

[12] Mabel Dodge Luhan, *Lorenzo in Taos,* Secker, 1933, pp. 230 ff.

> thy God, and thy God shall fall in. . . . And the world shall be godless, there shall no God walk on the mountains, no whirlwind shall stir like a heart in the deeps of the blue firmament. . . . [But] the Gods do not die. They go down a deep pit, and live on at the bottom of oblivion. And when a man staggers, he stumbles and falls backwards down the pit . . . where the gods of the past live on. And they laugh, and eat his soul.[13]

But against these—highly significant—ravings there is set the clear, fresh voice of David, singing: 'When I consider thy heavens, the work of thy fingers. . . . O Lord, our Lord, how excellent is thy name in all the earth! Who has set thy glory above the heavens.'

Were these gods altogether dead? That was the fundamental question. On his second visit to New Mexico Lawrence wrote the strange and powerful, but bi-valvular, novelette, *St Mawr* (1924). (Bi-valvular, because two-thirds of the way through he forgets all about the horse-hero, St Mawr himself, and becomes absorbed by New Mexico.) The little Welsh groom, Lewis (who is a first sketch, in some ways, for the 'Parkin' of the first version of *Lady Chatterley:* very different from the final 'Mellors' of the third version)[14] discusses God with Mrs Witt:

> I don't know about God. But when I see a star fall like that out of long-distant places in the sky: and the moon sinking, saying Good-bye! Good-bye! . . . I think I hear something, though I wouldn't call it God. . . . And you smell the smell of oak-leaves now, now the air is cold. They smell to me more alive than people. The trees hold their bodies hard and still, but they watch and listen with their leaves.

And when the novel moves away from Wales to the Mexican ranch at the end—and Lawrence's prose blossoms out marvellously, as usual for the occasion—we learn that

> There is no Almighty loving God. The God there is shaggy as the pine-trees, and horrible as the lightning.

[13] *David,* pp. 78 ff.

[14] See below, pp. 106 and 110 ff.

But if these gods are dead, or, as it seems, hibernating, can Lawrence bring them to life again? And the answer comes in the failure of *The Plumed Serpent.* We shall see below that, looking back in 1931, Lawrence did indeed regard his time in New Mexico as formative. But for the moment he is disillusioned. Back in Germany, after this return visit to Taos, he writes (1926): 'I am very much inclined to agree that one must look for real guts and self-responsibility to the Northern peoples.'[15] This—after all we have come to associate 'the North' with in Lawrence's vocabulary! It is not merely inconsistency. Of course Lawrence was one of the most happily inconsistent writers in all literature. But here it is a genuine conviction, now that he has come to believe that, fundamentally, America has failed him. Rather tentatively, he sees flashes of hope in sword-dancing, folk-music, open-air camps, in England and elsewhere. Yet he is too acute not to see that this may be mere faddism—'a sort of mummery'.[16] So that in the last resort he has now come to feel that the gods can only be resurrected through the intimate relationship of man and woman, through veneration of the phallus. Now his liturgy is no longer to be the hymns of Ramón but the incantations of 'John Thomas'.[17]

II

Strangely enough, it was old Edward Garnett who was perhaps ultimately to blame. In a letter to Garnett's son, David, about *Lady Chatterley,* Lawrence says, 'I should like to give your father a copy, if he'd care for it. . . . In my early days your father said to me, "I should welcome a description of the whole act"—which has stayed in my mind till I wrote this book.'[18] I think we must admit that the

[15] *Letters,* p. 666.
[16] *ibid.,* p. 700.
[17] Lawrence's nickname for the phallus in *Lady Chatterley.*
[18] *Letters* (1928), p. 746.

monotonous insistence upon the sex-act in the book is due, in part at least, to an (unconscious) compensatory expression of his own desire for emancipation. He is, of course, perfectly serious in the book. Indeed, its defect is that it is all too much in deadly earnest; Mellors himself has no real sense of humour, only a sardonic wit, and we are genuinely relieved when Connie (Lady Chatterley) gives a ' snirt ' of laughter at some of his more solemn pornographics. But all his friends have testified to the ' puritan ' in Lawrence. His own sister says, 'Bert would never tolerate vulgarity and dirty stories '.[19] The Brewsters say the same of him in later years: ' Never during my years of intimacy with him . . . have I ever known him to tell a vulgar story, nor to joke and speak lightly of sex, never have I known him to treat or regard human beings with less dignity or less delicacy than another. Indeed, he was the Puritan.'[20] Dorothy Brett describes Frieda and Lawrence arguing over James Joyce's *Ulysses,* and Lawrence saying vehemently, ' The last part of it is the dirtiest, most indecent, obscene thing ever written. Yes it is, Frieda. It is filthy.' And she also tells of how a man at Oaxaca, having heard of Lawrence's reputation, hands him a book, on the cover of which is the picture of a woman pulling off her chemise, a man in evening dress watching her. ' This is just the book for you ', the man says to Lawrence. Lawrence takes it in his hands, a look of astonishment on his face, holds it for a few moments in silence, and then hands it quietly back without saying a word.[21] Some of Lawrence's Bohemian friends, such as Peter Warlock, were astonished at Lawrence's sensitiveness. But Lawrence sometimes seems to express in prose what he represses in life. Knud Merrild

[19] Ada Lawrence and Stuart Gelder, *Early Life of D. H. Lawrence,* Secker, 1932, p. 51.

[20] E. and A. Brewster, *Reminiscences and Correspondence of D. H. Lawrence,* p. 122.

[21] Dorothy Brett, *Lawrence and Brett: A Friendship,* Secker, 1933, p. 79.

tells of a curious incident of Lawrence as they knew him in New Mexico. When a Miss Meta Lehmann came up to visit them on the ranch, and could not get back the same night, Lawrence was genuinely shocked at the idea that she should stay the night in the same house as the two young Danes, the artists—and became quite violent about it. Yet in one of his short stories, *The Fox,* Lawrence himself represents precisely the same dilemma, reversed—a young man, staying the night in the house with two young ladies. 'It wouldn't be improper, would it?' the young man asks. And they finally decide not to take any notice of what the village may say.[22] One cannot help feeling that at times in his writings Lawrence is trying to make up (so to speak) for leeway lost in his shielded, nonconformist upbringing.

Nevertheless the job needed doing. And misrepresentations of what Lawrence was after will not help. It is quite unfair to say for instance, as Mr Eric Bentley does, that 'Klage's vitalism ends like Lawrence's in blasphemy against life itself, and *Lady Chatterley's Lover* is a shocking book, not for what it mentions but for what it advocates.... The romantic quest for a life of sensations rather than thoughts reaches its culmination in a religion of sex and power, of his own John Thomas and Nietzsche's Dionysos.'[23] But this is not at all what Lawrence does 'advocate'. He is emphatic in his *A Propos of Lady Chatterley* that

> Far be it from me to suggest that all women should go running after game-keepers for lovers. Far be it from me to suggest that they should be running after anybody. A great many men and women today are happiest when they abstain and stay sexually apart, quite clean: and at the same time when they understand and realize sex more fully.[24]

And so we can take Mellors quite seriously when at the end of the novel, waiting for Connie to be able to come to him, he writes to her: 'I love being chaste now. I love it as

[22] 'The Fox' in *Tales,* Heinemann, 1934, p. 429.
[23] Eric Bentley, *Cult of the Superman,* p. 230.
[24] *A Propos of Lady Chatterley's Lover,* p. 15.

snowdrops love the snow. . . . Now is the time to be chaste, it is so good to be chaste, like a river of cool water in my soul.' Lawrence's loathing of indiscriminate sex relations arose partly, no doubt, from his upbringing. It is interesting that, discussing the effect of 'the pox' upon the consciousness of Europe from about the Elizabethan period onward, he remarks by the way, 'I have never had syphilis myself. Yet I know and confess how profound is my fear of the disease, and more than fear, my horror. In fact, I don't think I am so very much afraid of it. I am much more horrified, inwardly and deeply, at the idea of its existence.'[25] Of Casanova he said once, 'he smells. One can be immoral if one likes, but one must not be a creeping, itching, fingering, inferior being, led on chiefly by a dirty sniffing kind of curiosity.'[26] When first he went away with Frieda he wrote to Edward Garnett that 'Love is a much bigger thing than passion, and a woman much more than sex' (1912).[27] And in 1930 he reiterates, in 'We Need One Another'[28] that 'Sex, to me, means the whole of the relationship between man and woman'. At one moment we find him almost apologizing for his predominant preoccupation, in this novel, with the purely physical side of the relationship, and explaining that the two sides have come apart and that it is his vocation to bring them together again. 'It [*Lady Chatterley*] is a novel of the phallic consciousness . . . versus the mental-spiritual consciousness: and of course you know which side I take. The *versus* is not my fault. There should be no *versus*. The two things must be reconciled in us. But now they're daggers drawn.'[29] Indeed, his apologies for the novel are numerous.[30] But perhaps the best brief exposition is con-

[25] *Phoenix: Introduction to these Paintings* (1929), p. 555.
[26] *Letters* (1921), p. 523.
[27] *ibid.* (1912), p. 43.
[28] *Scribner's Magazine (Phoenix*, p. 194).
[29] E. and A. Brewster, *Reminiscences and Correspondence of D. H. Lawrence*, p. 166.
[30] *A Propos of Lady Chatterley's Lover;* the Introduction to the Paris Edition of *Lady Chatterley's Lover;* and *Pornography and So On.*

tained in a letter to Lady Ottoline Morrell (1928) in which he says:

> About *Lady C.*—you mustn't think I advocate perpetual sex. Far from it. Nothing nauseates me more than promiscuous sex in and out of season. But I want, with *Lady C.*, to make an *adjustment in consciousness* to the basic physical realities. . . . God forbid that I should be taken as urging loose sex activity. There is a brief time for sex, and a long time when sex is out of place. But when it is out of place as an activity there still should be the large and quiet space in the consciousness where it lives quiescent. Old people can have a lovely quiescent sort of sex, like apples, leaving the young free for their sort.[31]

In all this Lawrence seems to me much closer to the Christian view of sex, properly understood, than were many of his opponents (within and without the Church). The cynical, functional attitude that Lawrence was attacking appears to lie behind, for instance, the remarks about Lawrence in a recent book by Mr Rayner Heppenstall: 'Even Lawrence's private experience of sex must have been on occasion either comical or repulsive. . . . The truth is two-sided. Sometimes sex is awful, and sometimes it is funny. Rather occasionally, it is a clap of thunder and a revelation. At its married best, it is a gay, instructive, sensitizing and well-mannered game. It also is a means of generating children. . . .'[32] But Lawrence has already examined this view. In an article, 'Making Love to Music',[33] he says:

> Even a man like Maupassant, an apparent devotee of sex, says the same thing: . . . Surely, he says, the act of copulation is the Creator's cynical joke against us. To have created in us all these beautiful and noble sentiments of love, to set the nightingale and all the heavenly spheres singing, merely to throw us into this grotesque posture, to perform this humiliating act, is a piece of cynicism worthy of . . . a mocking demon.

[31] *Letters*, p. 773.
[32] R. Heppenstall, *The Double Image*, Secker, 1947, p. 61.
[33] *Phoenix*, pp. 160 ff.

And he introduces the same problem into *Lady Chatterley* itself: he shows us at one point how Connie, through looking on, as it were from the outside, critically and half-amusedly, at the physical act, reduces it in fact to a failure. It remains inoperative until she can accept it, humbly, thankfully, at bottom 'religiously'. And this surely coincides with the Christian view, according to which the physical is to be taken, wholly, gratefully, and offered to God in the very act. Lawrence saw this from time to time. In his story, *The Captain's Doll,* he explicitly quotes the phrase from the Anglican marriage service, ' To love and to cherish ', as exactly expressing what he means. And in his superb short story, 'Glad Ghosts', he enlarges on it. Luke, Lord Lathwill, is speaking to Col. Hale about the latter's late wife: ' You may have been awfully good to her. But her poor woman's body, were you ever good to that? . . . That's the point. If you understand the marriage service: with my body I thee worship. That's the point. No getting away from it.' But usually he was more conscious of a contradiction between his view and what he thought to be the Christian ' hush-hush ' view, the view that sex is a necessary evil, to be endured merely for the sake of procreation.

Unfortunately we must admit that there has been a strain in Catholic as well as Protestant teaching which has reduced sex to a mere implement, *concupiscentia* being regarded as *the* sign, because it happens also to be the channel, of original sin. We need only read some of the sermons (say) of St Bernard on chastity, or some of the theological discussions that went on in the twelfth and thirteenth centuries about the doctrine of the ' immaculate conception ' of the Blessed Virgin, to see that Mr C. S. Lewis is in the right when he declares that the scholastics were too concerned with sexual appetite and with marriage as guaranteeing the survival of the race to be much interested in love.[34] St Thomas Aquinas, more balanced than most, avoids a

[34] C. S. Lewis, *The Allegory of Love,* OUP, 1938, p. 16.

tendency to explicit Manicheeism, such as others seem to show. But in the article in his *Summa,* on *Utrum cognescens uxorem, non intendens aliquod bonum matrimonii, sed solam delectionem, mortaliter peccet,'*[35] he certainly seems to suggest that any ' enjoyment ' of the sexual act, which is not wholly and merely an ' enjoyment ' or ' delight ' in what will be the fruit of the act, is sin—indeed, is of the nature of mortal sin. In systematic terms, the difference between Lawrence's view and that of the medievals, is that according to the latter the evil in sexual relations lies in the *ligamentum rationis,* the suspension of intellectual activity: whereas for Lawrence this is its supreme significance. In fact, both are right, or at least each is needed to complete the other. Lawrence himself would have agreed that sex as pure sub-rational animality must be condemned (he condemns it himself by comparing it with the acts of puppydogs); on the other hand, the divorce of mind from body and the over-intellectualizing of the physical destroys the very unity of man for which the best of the scholastics were in other ways contending. It remains true that Lawrence rightly suspected (with no knowledge of traditional Catholic theology) that something was wrong in the balance of Christian teaching, especially as so often expounded in his day. And we have to thank him for re-emphasizing an element in the doctrine of Creation which has too often been neglected.

And it is, after all, very significant that Lawrence, in spite of his personal history, should come to defend so stoutly the necessity for fidelity. Few incidents are sadder to me than one recorded by Dorothy Brett. A group are talking in Taos one evening, and Lawrence starts passionately declaiming against divorce: ' very intense, very evangelic ', as he sometimes becomes when a subject moves him deeply, says Miss Brett. At last one of them observes: ' Isn't that funny, coming from you?' Lawrence looks surprised and asks 'Why?'

[35] *Summa Theologica* III Supp. xlix. 6; cf. I-II xxiv i ad i; III Supp. xxix 2, xli. 4, xlix, 4,5.

'Well,' she replies, 'you are staying in the house of one divorcee; you are visiting another; and you are married to another.' Lawrence looks at her for a moment; then suddenly drops his head. 'Yes, you are right,' he says, sadly and heavily.[36] Earlier he had toyed with other ideas. In 1916 he writes in a way which seems to advocate polygamy for some people;[37] and in *The Boy in the Bush* he shows us (or at least allows his co-author, Miss Skinner, to show us) Jack hankering after two wives and annoyed because Mary won't consent to his being shared with Monica! Some have even accused Lawrence of advocating homosexuality. It is true that at one time (*e.g.*, in *Women in Love*) he talked about the necessity of having a man-to-man relationship to complete the man-to-woman relationship. But the relations of Cyril and George (*The White Peacock*), Birkin and Gerald (*Women in Love*), Lilly and Aaron (*Aaron's Rod*), or Ramón and Cipriano (*The Plumed Serpent*) are emphatically not those of perverts. The 'pervert' chapter in *The Rainbow* is called 'Shame'. And Knud Merrild's comments on Lawrence's own personal attitude and constitution are, I think, final.[38] At any rate, Lawrence became increasingly clear of the fact of marriage as a permanent, valid thing. Until he can declare, in the famous words of *A Propos Lady Chatterley:*

> The Church is established upon a recognition of some, at least, of the greatest and deepest desires in man. . . . And the Church, celibate as its priesthood may be, built as it may be upon the lonely rock of Peter, or of Paul, really rests upon the indissolubility of marriage. Make marriage in any serious degree unstable, dissoluble, destroy the permanence of marriage, and the Church falls. Witness the enormous decline of the Church of England. . . . Perhaps the greatest contribution to the social life of man made by Christianity is—marriage. . . . And the Church created marriage by making it a sacrament, a sacrament of man and woman united in the sex

[36] Dorothy Brett, *Lawrence and Brett: A Friendship*, pp. 127 ff.
[37] *Letters*, pp. 323 ff.
[38] Knud Merrild, *A Poet and Two Painters*, pp. 103 ff, 208.

communion, and never to be separated, except by death.... Marriage, making one complete body out of two incomplete ones, and providing for the complex development of the man's soul and woman's soul in unison, throughout a lifetime.

III

The novel, therefore, was written with a solemn purpose, a sort of divine vocation. And this constitutes its main weakness, though it is less blatantly didactic than *The Plumed Serpent*. It is interesting that, to some critics at least, the third and published draft is much more self-conscious and artificial than the first draft. Frieda herself preferred the first draft, and said that in the final draft he had wanted to sharpen up the contrast between the cynicism and sophistication of the modern mind and the gamekeeper's own attitude. He did this by turning the original Parkin, a real, simple, comic, natural, rather ferrety-looking working man, reminiscent of Lewis (in *St Mawr*) or of Cicio (in *The Lost Girl*), into the more educated but humourless and boring Mellors. In the first version Lady Chatterley 'thought of Parkin and the soft dilation of passion in his eyes, with those quick, quivering lights.... When the keeper's eyes dilated and became full of soft, flashing lightning, she felt so real, so real.'[39] Mellors is never described thus, and talks a great deal more than Parkin. There is 'outspokenness' in the first version, but it is not so deliberately provocative as the final version so often seems to make it—there seems to be little doubt that as time went on, and as opposition to publication of the novel increased, Lawrence became more and more determined to say the worst that could be said in print; and hence the rather monotonous, cloying insistence of the final version. There is, it goes without saying, fine prose in both. Take this passage, which occurs only in the first draft:

[39] Edited by Esther Forbes, Phoenix Pub. Co. Ltd., Scherz & Hallwag, Paris (n.d.) pp. 75 and 85.

> She [Connie] felt herself filled with new blood, as if the blood of the man had swept into her veins like a strong, fresh, rousing wind, changing her whole self. All her self felt alive, and in motion, like the woods in spring. . . . All her body felt like the dark interlacing of the boughs of an oak wood, softly humming in a wind, and humming inaudibly with the myriad, myriad unfolding of buds. Meanwhile the birds had their heads laid on their shoulders and slept with delight in the vast interlaced intricacy of the forest of her body. . . .[40]

And Connie herself is somewhat altered in the final version; it is a little extravagant to call her there a 'nymphomaniac', as Miss Forbes does,[41] but it is true that the indiscriminacy of her early sexual relations in this final version (which is absent from the first) does undermine our belief in her attainment of harmony and fidelity with Mellors. And yet, with all these weaknesses, even the final version of *Lady Chatterley* is a wonderful achievement.

There is an interesting anticipation of one element in the novel, in the story of *The Virgin and the Gipsy*. The girl, Yvette, gets to know the gipsy (who later rescues her, and has intercourse with her, in the flood) and discusses him with a Major Eastwood who, it happens, knew the gipsy in his regiment during the war. 'That gipsy,' he muses, 'was the best man we had, with horses. Nearly died of pneumonia. I thought he *was* dead. He's a resurrected man to me.' Now Mellors, too, had been a blacksmith to the cavalry in Egypt; he got his commission, but, like the gipsy, fell ill in the Army. And though his body contains inner power, it is outwardly thin and delicate. The point seems to be this: a 'resurrected' man is somehow different from the ordinary run of men, therefore he is privileged to act in ways which would not be permissible to most. Therefore there is no contradiction between Lawrence's defence

40 *ibid.*, p. 64.
41 *ibid.* 'MS Report' by Esther Forbes. (She received the MS from Mrs Lawrence, via Willard Houghland, Assistant to the Director, Laboratory of Anthropology, Santa Fé).

of fidelity and anti-promiscuity and his picture of a gamekeeper who commits adultery with the wife of his employer. This is to adopt something like Kierkegaard's famous claim for the 'teleological suspension of morality'. Or rather, Lawrence re-defines morality in his own way. And that way is essentially religious, almost mystical. The greatness of sex lies in its mystery. We can't get away from the 'dirty little secret' view of sex by 'being wise and scientific about it like Dr Marie Stopes: though to be wise and scientific . . . is better than to be utterly hypocritical'. But the danger is that we may 'kill dynamic sex altogether, and leave only the scientific and deliberate mechanism'. The only way out is for man to 'come to the limits of himself and become aware of something beyond him . . . to be aware of that which surpasses him'.[42] And that is the religious view.

This is the only way in which *Lady Chatterley's Lover* is really bearable. As a story in the 'realist' tradition it is merely dull, apart from such excitation as the pornographic passages may have for this or that reader. (How dull, the expurgated edition reveals.) To so many people these are the passages which alone matter and for which the book is procured. But read as a great symbolic drama, with a vast religious theme supported by its own ritual and liturgy, it is very powerful. Lawrence was a supreme ritualist, and most successful, not when he was trying to ape ecclesiastical ritual (as in the dressing-up scenes in *The Plumed Serpent,* which are merely rather comic and sententious) but when he is treating nature ritually. Think, for instance, of the rhythmic movements in *The Rainbow,* when Anna and Will are harvesting and move nearer and nearer to each other as they set down their shocks, till the moment when the rows meet and they meet in love; or of Anna's naked dancing to the Lord when she is with child; or of Gudrun's queer eurhythmic dancing before the cows in *Women in Love;* or of the solemn Mexican dances in *The Plumed Serpent* and

[42] *Pornography and Obscenity* in *Phœnix,* 1929, p. 182.

elsewhere; and then of Connie's wild dancing in the wood in the rain. There is the ritual. And the liturgy: compare the movement of the prose in these two passages. The first is from the famous opening of *The Rainbow:*

> They felt the rush of the sap in spring, they knew the wave which cannot halt, but every year throws forward the seed to begetting, and, falling back, leaves the young-born on the earth. They knew the intercourse between heaven and earth, sunshine drawn into the breast and bowels, the rain sucked up in the daytime, nakedness that comes under the wind in autumn, showing the birds' nests no longer worth hiding. . . . The young corn waved and was silken, and the lustre slid along the limbs of the men who saw it. They took the udder of the cows, the cows yielded milk and pulse against the hands of the men, the pulse of the blood of the teats of the cows beat into the pulse of the hands of the men. . . .

The second is from *Lady Chatterley:*

> And it seemed she was like the sea, nothing but dark waves rising and heaving, heaving with a great swell, so that slowly her whole darkness was in motion, and she was ocean rolling its dark, dumb mass. Oh, and far down inside her the deeps parted and rolled asunder, in long, far-travelling billows, and ever, at the quick of her, the depths parted and rolled asunder, from the centre of soft plunging . . . and further and further rolled the waves of herself away from herself, leaving her, till suddenly, in a soft, shuddering convulsion, the quick of her plasm was touched, she knew herself touched, the consummation was upon her, and she was gone. She was gone, she was not, and she was born: a woman.[43]

It is magnificent. In each case the prose takes on the very rhythm of the actions it is describing: and there is about it the solemnity, almost, of a chant. But it is not far from the point of becoming *récitatif*. Sometimes his poetry actually reaches that point. Compare with the above the long, sinuous, rhythmic hymns of Ramón:

> When the dream of the eyes is darkened, and encompassed
> with Now.

[43] cap. xii, p. 181.

And the dream of the mouth resounds the last I Am.
And the dream of the hands is a sleep like a bird on the sea, that sleeps and is lifted and shifted, and knows not.
And the dreams of the feet and the toes touch the core of the world where the Serpent sleeps.

(*The Plumed Serpent*)

The movement is irresistible, but the words—they have become magic sounds only, hypnotic, almost dervish.

Of course not all *Lady Chatterley* is of this kind. There is some excellent characterization—Mrs Bolton, Sir Clifford himself, or the brief sketch of Connie's racy father, a fine bawdy aristocrat (a recapitulation, as Horace Gregory points out, of Sir William Franks in *Aaron's Rod*). Moreover, on the whole there is much less of Lawrence's tendency to bombast and repetition than in (say) *The Plumed Serpent*. And above all, the exquisite sensitiveness to places and prospects and history has returned from its exile abroad to give us the very pulse of England, this central England, dying of industrialism and impotence, and yet still with its warm powers of recuperation. Can we not, then, just take the novel for these things, and for its quiet and essentially *hopeful* close (Connie expecting her child, and more sure of Mellors than Alvina ever really was of Cicio in *The Lost Girl*)? (See p. 67 *sup.*) Can we accept these things as part of a great symbolic drama, of which the phallus is really the hero, twentieth-century cerebralness and sterility the villain, and all the characters merely shadowy chorus?

I fear the answer is: Not quite. It is precisely the so often realist technique that makes it impossible. We may try willingly to suspend our disbelief. But it returns, telling us for instance that Mellors would have a Christian name (it is only mentioned twice in the novel—Oliver; otherwise he is ' the gamekeeper ' or ' he ' or, rarely, ' Mellors '); that he would not so easily slip from intelligent Lawrentian discussion to the Derbyshire brogue (Parkin, in the first version, is more consistent and never abandons the brogue). Nor can we believe that Connie, so free of her body with other lovers, would then so easily be able to achieve this perfect, stable relationship with Mellors (in the first version, again as we saw above, this problem does not arise). Least of all can we believe that Lawrence's picture of Mellors and his 'tenderness' is compatible with that 'short summer night' (chapter sixteen) before Connie goes to Italy, when we are told, vaguely, that 'she learnt so much.' The 'perversions' that are, delicately, hinted at in this demurely allusive passage, are, we cannot help but feel, psychological deviations which do not match with the 'sanctified sensuality' of the rest of the relationship. The evasiveness of the description gives the case away.

IV

There is one influence upon Lawrence which has, so far as I know, hardly ever been mentioned: Vasili Vasilievich Rozanov. Rozanov was the famous Russian exponent of 'pan-sexualism', and Lawrence himself reviewed two of his books and notes (1930) that he 'is acquiring something of a European reputation. There is a translation in French, and one promised in German, and the advanced young writers in Paris and Berlin talk of him as one of the true lights.'[44] His review of *Solitaria* appeared in 1927. But it seems to me most likely that he was influenced long before that. He had, after all, been a friend of S. S. Koteliansky for many years, and had written an Introduction back in 1920 to "Kot's" translation of *All Things Are Possible* by Leo Shestov.[45] It would be interesting to know at what date Koteliansky came to know the works of Rozanov, and

[44] Review of Rozanov, *Fallen Leaves* (Everyman, Jan. 23, 1930), reprinted in *Phoenix*, p. 340. More about Rozanov may be found in N. Berdyaev, *The Russian Idea*, Bles, 1947.
[45] See below, p. 152.

whether he spoke much to Lawrence about them. The *prima facie* evidence is that he did.[46]

For there are quite remarkable correspondences, as well as highly significant differences. Rozanov was born in 1856, and was among other things a teacher. In 1880 he married Mlle Souslov, Dostoevsky's mistress (the original of Princess Nastasya in *The Idiot*). His book *Solitaria* was suppressed by the censor as anti-Christian and pornographic. Towards the end of his life he became extremely pious and a strong supporter of the old régime. He was arrested by the Bolshevists in 1918, and his last letters were written from prison; he received the last sacraments and passed away during reading of the prayers for the dying on January 23, 1919. Lawrence does see in him a kindred spirit. Especially in his 'The Apocalypse of Our Times' (appended to *Solitaria*), Lawrence sees 'the genuine pagan vision, the phallic vision', and says that for the first time we get in Rozanov, 'what we have got from no Russian, neither Tolstoi nor Dostoievsky nor any of them, a real, positive view on life. . . . He is the first Russian, as far as I am concerned, who has ever said anything to me. And his vision is full of passion, vivid, valid. He is the first to see that immortality is in the vividness of life, not in the loss of life.'[47] What then does Rozanov say? As he is very little known in this country, I will give fairly extensive quotations from Koteliansky's translations of the two works available in English.

> God as it were pointed out to man for ever and anon where it is possible to meet him. 'Look for me not in the woods nor in the fields, nor in the wilderness, not on the peak of the mountain, nor in the valley below, nor in the waters, nor under the earth—but . . . *where* I made a covenant with Abraham your father.' . . . Astonishing. . . . But in that case, how understandable it becomes why asexualists are at the same time atheists.[48]

[46] See above, p. 16.
[47] Review of Rozanov, *Solitaria ibid.*, p. 370.
[48] *Solitaria,* translated by Koteliansky (Wishart, 1927), p. 93.

In the following quotation Koteliansky seems to have been influenced in his translation by Lawrence's own terminology:

> I boundlessly love human *connectedness*, people in connection, in mutual fondling, caressing.... I hate nothing so much and am most hostile to everything that *separates* people, that prevents them from *fusing*, being *connected*, 'becoming one flesh'.[49]

> From (the) *composition of life* how evident it becomes that our *genitalia* are more important than our brain.[50]

> Christ certainly knew all this [*sc.* about the phallic cults] ... and it was enough for Him to aphallicize Himself and religion in order to destroy religion altogether, its very essence, its source, the Tree of Life (= phallus).... Generally from the *text* of the Gospels there naturally emerges the monastery. The monastery, avitalism....[51]

(Could this, perhaps, have originally given Lawrence the idea which he worked up into 'The Escaped Cock' or 'The Man Who Died'?) And consider Rozanov's reply to the censor, when his *In the World of the Indefinite and the Unsolved* was suppressed:

> The religion of 'the opening bud' is the complete denial—a denial to the very root, and to the end of time—of pornography, a complete denial of the bourgeois and low, salacious and hooliganish attitude towards sex.... The same thing is done in marriage and in a 'gay house', but again what a difference! Society, the public, the critics, finally the official censorship cannot and do not wish to distinguish that difference, and they accuse me of talking of a 'brothel' when I am speaking of the Egyptian 'bud' (marriage).[52]

And might not this have come straight out of Lawrence:

[49] *ibid.*, p. 103.
[50] *ibid.*, p. 112.
[51] *The Apocalypse of our Time* (included in same vol. with *Solitaria*, p. 178).
[52] *ibid.* (quot. from E. Gollerbach, *Critico-Biographical Study*, p. 16; abridged translation of his *Life and Works of V. V. Rozanov*, Petersburg, 1922).

Paganism is morning. Christianity—evening.[53]

Or:

From my childhood I never liked to read the Gospels. It did not attract me. . . . Of the Old Testament, on the contrary, I could never have enough: everything there seemed to me *truth* and extraordinarily *warm*, precisely as though in the words and lines *blood is flowing*, one's own blood! [54]

I was agitated and attracted, rather fascinated by breasts and by a pregnant belly. I constantly desired to see the whole world pregnant. . . . The interest in the ' belly ' instantly removes partitions, distances. . . . This tremendous unifying, socializing role of the belly is astounding, moving, noble, lofty. From the ' belly ' come just as many ideas as from the head (which is fairly empty).[55]

But there is another element in Rozanov which we miss in Lawrence, and it is the element which, I believe, finally brings him a unification of his ideas without losing the force of what he has been asserting before.

The soul of Orthodoxy is in the gift of prayer. Its body is—the rites, the cult. . . . He who loves the Russian people can't help loving the Church too. For the people and the Church are one.[56]

The extraordinary *power* of the Church arises (among other things) from this that people come to her *in the very best moments* of their life and soul: painful, sad, terrible, pathetic moments. . . . The church captures the ' fringes of all hearts ': and there is no other place of such potency as this.[57]

And finally a passage expressing the attitude for which Lawrence most strongly criticizes Rozanov:

[53] *Fallen Leaves,* Bundle One, 1913 (translated by Koteliansky, Mandrake Press, n.d., p. 40).
[54] *ibid.*, p. 79.
[55] *ibid.*, p. 92.
[56] *Solitaria,* p. 119.
[57] *Fallen Leaves*, p. 115.

> How hollow is my rebellion against Christianity. I ought to have lived a good life, and I had been given (for twenty years) very favourable conditions. . . .
>
> The Church is the only poetic, the only profound thing on earth. God, what madness it was that for eleven years I made every possible effort to destroy the Church. And how fortunate that I failed. What would the *earth* be like without the Church? It would suddenly lose its meaning and get cold.[58]

There is, in fact, in the last resort something slightly thin and cold about Lawrence's sexualism which Rozanov, living in an older and a wiser tradition, was able to transcend. Lawrence somewhere observes that the genuine Byzantine Christianity is ' incomprehensible ' to him. And so it was, in spite of moments of real insight. It is significant, I think, that Lawrence was so insistent on disentangling the phallic reality from any mere utilitarian purpose that he goes to the opposite extreme of excluding the reproductive instinct from it altogether. Some of his women characters want, and have, children. But Cicio (in *The Lost Girl*) is the only Lawrentian hero I can think of who positively desires his wife to bear his children. (We remember the comic note in *St Mawr*, that the stallion had no foals—at least, till it disappears in Mexico—' because it did not want to '!) The result is an unreal insulation of the sex act from the total natural scheme. It is true that Lawrence has an extraordinary penetration into child-being—witness the description of the fighting youngsters in Annable's cottage (*The White Peacock*), the superb passage in *The Rainbow* where young Anna Lensky gradually overcomes her suspicions of her stepfather, or the brilliant account of the little girl's illness in *England, my England!* And his remarks about education and child-upbringing (*e.g.*, in *Fantasia* or in *The Education of the People*[59]) are full of good sense. It is significant too

[58] *Solitaria*, p. 139.
[59] Unpublished: originally written for The *Times Educational Supplement* (*Phoenix*, pp. 587 ff).

that, unlike many novels of the 'twenties and 'thirties, contraceptive devices do not seem to figure in Lawrence's stories. (Mellors asks whether Connie has taken any precautions against having a child. 'No,' she says faintly, 'I should hate that.'[60]) Yet the gravamen still remains: that it is not really the whole man and the whole woman that Lawrence finally produces for us, though he gets nearer to it than any other novelist, except perhaps Thomas Mann, of his time. And the reason is, surely, his failure to resurrect the gods of man and woman. This is why, as most critics feel, there is a sadness hanging around his greatest attempt to do so, *Lady Chatterley's Lover*. The sadness is not merely at the 'failure' of the novelist, or the preacher's anti-climax: it is that the little boat on which he sails this novel will not bear the weight of the world's future which is to be its cargo. In other words, that the 'objective correlative' to Lawrence's particular emotional experience behind the writing of the novel is too flimsy to convey it. And yet, for my part, I believe it to be a book for which we ought to be profoundly grateful, though it is not, by far, his greatest, and though as art it is a beautiful cul-de-sac. If it is a cul-de-sac, it is so only because he fails to persuade us that the dead gods can really be resuscitated down this road.

[60] *Lady Chatterley's Lover*, cap. xii, p. 176.

CHAPTER FIVE

RESURRECTION

I

THE sadness that many critics have felt, in reading *Lady Chatterley's Lover,* is, I believe, basically due to the conviction that Lawrence was there trying to do two things at once and failing. He had argued that the physical, sensual, and psychological impotence of our civilization was due to a decline in religious belief—belief in the 'dark gods'. But then he tries to restore the gods by reviving the vital phallic relation of man and woman. This is like trying to cure a cancer by prescribing gymnastic exercises: the inability to do exercises may be a symptom of cancer, and cure of the cancer may restore the ability; but the cancer cannot be cured *by* the exercises. If this is so, then the failure, such as it is, of *Lady Chatterley* as a novel, is symptomatic of the failure of Lawrence himself as artist and as 'prophet', or, to use Mr Eliot's word, as 'medicine man'.

It is worth looking at Mr Eliot's indictment for a moment. 'I find', he says of Lawrence, 'the medicine man more important than the artist. . . . I think of Lawrence . . . as a researcher into religious emotion. . . . Lawrence had a really extraordinary capacity for being exacerbated by the modern world of enlightenment and progress. . . . This world was his nightmare; he wanted a world in which religion would be real, not a world of church congresses and religious newspapers, not even a world in which a religion could be *believed,* but a world in which religion would be something deeper than belief, in which life would be a kind of religious behaviourism. Hence the prancing Indians, who, in *Mornings in Mexico,* inspired some of his finest and most brilliant writing. He wished to go as low as possible in the scale of human consciousness, in order to find something that he could assure himself was real. The attempt is fundamentally chimerical. . . . He merely gives a marvellous record of how the Indians affect Lawrence.'[1]

Now, if we liked to adopt an extreme relativistic epistemology, we could, I suppose, say this of any historical or descriptive record. But it ought to be pointed out that Lawrence was well aware of the dangers of subjectivism. In *Mornings in Mexico* he says emphatically that 'White people always, or nearly always, write sentimentally about the Indians. . . . You can detest the insidious devil for having an utterly different way from our own great way. Or you can perform the mental trick, and fool yourself and others into believing that the befeathered and bedaubed darling is nearer to the true ideal gods than we are.'[2] Mabel Luhan is not always to be trusted, no doubt; but she did know her New Mexican Indians, and she does talk of ' that wonderful, deeply understanding description of the dance ', and says that in these essays on the Indians Lawrence did ' capture a few fragments of a cosmos that he barely glimpsed . . .'[3]—most of which he learned from Tony Luhan, her Indian husband, whom Lawrence really does seem to have comprehended. And it was several years later, after cool reflection, that Lawrence could write:

> I think New Mexico was the greatest experience from the outside world that I have ever had. It certainly changed me for ever. . . . Months spent in holy Kandy, in Ceylon, the holy of holies of southern Buddhism, had not touched the great psyche of materialism-idealism which dominated me. And years, even in the exquisite beauty of Sicily, right among the old Greek paganism that still lives there, had not shattered the essential Christianity on which my character

[1] T. S. Eliot, in *Revelation,* ed. Baillie and Martin, Faber, 1937, pp. 30 ff.
[2] *Mornings in Mexico,* Secker, 1928, pp. 100 ff.
[3] M. D. Luhan, *Lorenzo in Taos,* pp. 230, 244.

> was established. . . . Tahiti, in a mere glimpse, repelled me: and so did California, after a stay of a few weeks. . . . But the moment I saw the brilliant, proud morning shine high up over the desert of Santa Fé, something stood still in my soul, and I started to attend. . . . I had no permanent feeling of religion till I came to New Mexico and penetrated into the old human race-experience there. . . . The Red Indian seems to me much older than the Greeks, or Hindus or any Europeans or even Egyptians. The Red Indian, as a civilized and truly religious man, civilized beyond taboo and totem, as he is in the south, is religious in perhaps the oldest sense, and deepest, of the word. . . . It is the religion which precedes the god-concept, and is therefore greater and deeper than any god-religion.[4]

There is one aspect, however, of Mr Eliot's criticism which is very cogent. In the same passage he observes, of Lawrence's strange personal life: 'The truth is, of course, that an artist needs to live a commonplace life if he is to get his work done'. Perhaps Lawrence would have been better—less dissipated, less turgid and repetitious—as an artist, if his life had been more controlled, more unified. He was, of course, in most senses of that abused word, a romantic. Writing to Murry in 1923, he says, 'This classiosity is bunkum, but still more, *cowardice*',[5] and Mr Murry's *Reminiscences* shows that the reference is to Mr Eliot himself. (Elsewhere he places the same writer in strange company: 'All the Lynds and Squires and Eliots and Goulds instinctively dislike [me]'!)[6] But at least he had not the romantic conception of artistic 'self-expression'. Mr Eliot's famous definition, 'Poetry is not a turning loose of emotion, but an escape from emotion; it is not the expression of personality, but an escape from personality', finds an echo, not only in Lawrence's movement away from the personal element in the novel, but even in some of his specific remarks about composition. As early as 1913, speaking

[4] 'New Mexico', in *Phoenix*, pp. 134 f.
[5] *Letters*, p. 578.
[6] *ibid.*, p. 801.

of *Sons and Lovers,* he writes: 'One sheds one's sicknesses in books—repeats and presents again one's emotions, to be master of them'.[7]

II

The mention of sickness is relevant at this point. Lawrence always deliberately moved out from himself as centre, to the world around—'Bishop Berkeley is absolutely right', he once observed: 'things only exist in our consciousness'.[8] And the fact that he himself was much subject to illness is quite as significant in Lawrence as in Keats or Kafka or any other tubercular artist. Not only are the descriptions of illness remarkably done—and still more the descriptions of recovery from illness. More, there is a distinctive quality given to life from the very fact that it moves, in his case, so constantly near to the margin of death. There is a fine account, for instance, in *The Ladybird,* of Count Dionys' sickness. We remember, too, the meaning of the Gipsy's and of Mellor's sickness; of Birkin's, of Lilly's; or of Kangaroo's struggle with death as the accompaniment of struggle for Somers' love. But there is one less-known instance which is worth pausing over: the illness of Jack in *Boy in the Bush.* We do not know exactly how much of this novel is by Lawrence, but I think it is a mistake to say, with Dr Leavis, that there is very little of him in it. The recorded facts are that a Miss M. L. Skinner, whom Lawrence met in Australia and advised about a manuscript of hers (Lawrence was most generous in his willingness to help young writers whom he thought any good), sent him the MS of another novel when he was in Mexico. Lawrence re-wrote it, keeping to the plot but working up the character of Jack, who in her version remained somewhat static throughout, altering the end, and adding passages of his own. It was

[7] *ibid.,* p. 150.
[8] 'On Being a Man', *Assorted Articles,* Secker, 1930, p. 192.

then published under their joint names. We learn from Dorothy Brett's Memoir that Frieda preferred an earlier version in which Jack does not die; but it is implied that this version too is Lawrence's. We can usually tell from the style which are most likely to be Lawrence's own passages; and Knud Merrild has identified a number of passages which reproduce actual experiences of Lawrence's in Mexico. It is safe, therefore, to say that the account of Jack's sickness is by Lawrence. Jack goes very near death, but ' would come back again, with a strange, haunted look in his blood-shot eyes '. And then, a little later:

> The two are never separate, life and death. And in the vast dark kingdom of the afterwards, the Lord of Death is the Lord of Life, and the God of Life and creation is Lord of death. . . . Unless Life moves on to the beauty of the darkness of death, there is no life, there is only automatism. Unless we see the dark splendour of death ahead, and travel to be lords of darkness at last, peers in the realms of death, our life is nothing but a petulant, pitiful backing, like a frightened horse, back, back, back to the stable, the manger, the cradle. But onward ahead is the great porch of the entry into death, with its columns of bone-ivory. . . .

The novel is not altogether satisfactory—a sort of blend of Faulkner and Nietzsche—but it does at times capture the queer, evasive mystery of life in the Bush and the intimate relation of sickness, death, and life. It is interesting to find Lawrence writing to Miss Skinner a year later, expressing sympathy over the death of her brother: ' And after all he lived his life and had his mates wherever he went. What more does a man want? So many old bourgeois people live on and on, and can't die, because they have never been in life at all. Death's not sad, when one has lived. . . .'[9] As he wrote once to Lady Asquith, ' only the dead are real '.[10] And not only real: in relation. He had hoped that Katherine Mansfield would live to read the *Fantasia;* when he learned

[9] *Letters,* p. 638.
[10] *ibid.,* p. 366.

she was dead, he wrote to Murry 'She'll know, though. The dead don't die. They look on and help.'[11] His wife reports him as saying, about 1923, 'The background of death is always there and the span of life is felt as fierce action. Life is only life when death is a part of it. Not like the Christian conception that shuts death away from life and says death comes after: death is always there.'[12] (This shows a significant ignorance of Christian 'eschatology'.)[13] Towards the end of his life, as his sicknesses grew worse, he wrote of suffering:

> The things that seemed to make up one's life die into insignificance, and the whole state is wretched. I've been through it these last three years—suffered, I tell you. But now I feel I'm coming through, to some other kind of happiness. It's a different kind of happiness we've got to come through to—but while the old sort is dying, and nothing new has appeared, it's really torture. . . . But we shall come through, and be really peaceful and in touch.[14]

And one of the loveliest things he ever wrote—or rather, dictated from his sick-bed—is the unfinished story, *The Flying Fish,*[15] of which he said that the last part was to have been 'regenerate man, a real life in this Garden of Eden'; but added, 'I've an intuition I shall not finish that novel. It was written so near the borderline of death, that I have never been able to carry it through, in the cold light of day.'[16]

III

It is out of this movement between life and death, where the human frame is ever shown to be at the mercy of the

[11] *ibid.*, p. 563.
[12] Frieda Lawrence, *Not I but the Wind,* Secker, 1935, p. 140.
[13] *cf.* p. 132 f below.
[14] Lawrence and Gelder, *Early Life of D. H. Lawrence,* p. 156.
[15] *Phoenix,* pp. 780 ff.
[16] E. and A. Brewster, *Reminiscences and Correspondence of D. H. Lawrence,* p. 288.

disintegrating powers of its physical nature—revealed, that is, in its fragility—and yet bravely fights its way back to living, that Lawrence evolves his whole theory of being. The process happens at crucial stages in a man's history; but it also happens, in a lesser degree, through the daily rhythm of sleep and waking. This is the meaning of strange pronouncements like

> You must start every single day fresh from the source. You must rise every day afresh out of the dark sea of the blood. When you go to sleep at night you have to say: 'Here dies the man I am and know myself to be.' And when you rise in the morning you have to say: 'Here rises an unknown quantity which is still myself.'[17]

Hence, too, comes the stress on 'mindlessness', hence the return to the 'dark gods', hence the 'savage pilgrimage'—to Ceylon, Australia, New Mexico, Old Mexico, the Etruscan Places, and (in imagination) Egypt and West Africa. And out of all that Lawrence develops a quite extraordinary sense of interrelation: interrelation between man and man, between man and animals, man and things. Things (a rock, a tree) are presented animistically (there should be a word 'animystically'.) Snakes, birds, cats, cows, all seem to have a consciousness of man's presence, and by their confronting him to restore man to his true place in the order of being. Horses perhaps above all. Dr W. Y. Tindall's somewhat learned *D. H. Lawrence and Susan his Cow*[18] excavates Lawrence's writing to find the Sacred Cow at the base of his philosophy. 'D. H. Lawrence and Stampede his Horse' would be a better field for research. Cicio observes: 'In England horses live a long time, because they *don't* live—never alive—see? In England railway-engines are alive, and horses go on wheels.'[19] In *The Boy in the Bush* Jack and Stampede almost become a centaur between them:

[17] *Fantasia*, p. 165.
[18] W. Y. Tindall, *D. H. Lawrence and Susan, his Cow, passim.*
[19] *Lost Girl*, p. 156.

What he [Jack] depended on was that bit of response the animal was capable of. . . . The boy balanced on the trembling, spurting stallion, looking down at it with dark-blue, wide, dark-looking eyes, and thinking of nothing, yet feeling so much; his face looking soft and warm with a certain masterfulness that was more animal than human, like a centaur, as if he were one blood with the horse.

It would be wearisome to note all the equine symbolism, and in any case Mr H. Gregory has given some space to this. But let us cite one final passage, from Lawrence's last prose work, *Apocalypse:*

Horses, always horses! How the horse dominated the mind of the early races, especially of the Mediterranean! . . . Far back, far back in our soul the horse prances . . . he is the beginning even of our godhead in the flesh. And as a symbol he roams the dark underworld meadows of the soul. . . . He stamps and threshes in the dark fields of your soul and mine.[20]

There is the same ' empathy ' behind the brilliant brief sketches Lawrence occasionally throws out with a flick of the wrist.

Gudrun came dressed in startling colours, like a macaw, when the family was in mourning. [Gerald] watched the lingering way she took her feet from the ground. And her ankles were pale yellow, and her dress a deep blue. . . . He felt the challenge in her very attire—she challenged the whole world. And he smiled as to the note of a trumpet.

Or this, from *Aaron's Rod:*

Aaron talked to an old, old Italian elegant in his side-curls, who peeled off his grey gloves and studied his formalities with a delightful mid-Victorian dash, and told stories about a *plaint* which Lady Surrey had against Lord Marsh, and was quite unintelligible. Out rolled the English words, like plums out of a burst bag, all completely unintelligible.

The point is that here are not merely ' vivid similes ', as in any novelist writing for effect, but a way of seeing the

[20] *Apocalypse,* p. 150.

togetherness of things: and thereby also, a way of trying to restore the relation between things sundered.

And surely Lawrence was right, that they were—and still are—sundered. He may have lacked both the philosophical and the psychological technical equipment to express his analysis. But he was not unaware of what the professionals were saying. He was one of the first to see the importance of psychological interpretations of our epoch such as are to be found in, for instance, Dr Trigant Burrow's work; and in letters to Dr Burrow, and the review he wrote of his *The Social Basis of Consciousness,* we find Lawrence not only restating Burrow's thesis in mercifully readable style, but finding professional confirmation for what he has observed all along:

> In the criticism of the Freudian method, Dr Burrow found, in his clinical experiences, that he was always applying a *theory*. . . . And gradually Dr Burrow realized that to fit life every time to a theory is in itself a mechanistic process, a process . . . of image-substitution. . . .
>
> The real trouble (the neurosis of modern life) lies in the inward sense of 'separateness' which dominates every man. At a certain point in his evolution, man became cognitively conscious. . . . Up till that time his consciousness flowed unawares, as in the animals. Suddenly his consciousness split. . . . [So] man is a prey to the division inside himself. Helplessly he must strive for more consciousness, which means, also, a more intensified aloneness, and a blind, dim yearning for the old togetherness of the far past, . . . the pre-conscious state.[21]

The thesis (in Dr Burrow's terms, in Dr Jung's or in others') is more familiar today than it was when Lawrence wrote. Philosophers and theologians are to a surprising degree stating (no doubt, in more careful language) what Lawrence saw by intuition. Those who have read, for instance, M. Berdyaev's essay on 'Solitude and Society',

[21] Review in American *Bookman,* 1927, *Phoenix,* p. 377.

or Dr Martin Buber's essay on 'Man,'[22] or some of the works of the Catholic philosopher, M. Gabriel Marcel, will recognize accounts which in some ways are very kindred to Lawrence's. M. Gabriel Marcel, for instance, in discussing the dangers of 'objectification', notes that 'The inability to perform correctly an habitual movement when I fix my attention on it, seems to show that my body only plays its rôle perfectly to the extent that I do not try to think of it itself as an object. My community with my body is indiscerptible.'[23] In the incident we quoted from *Lady Chatterley*, we found Lawrence applying the same argument to the sex-act: here, he might have said, is the supreme case of the impossibility of objectifying my body. I must act along with, or through, my body; if I try to stand outside it and direct it like a tool, it will not function properly. And the same is true of all human activity: the purely 'ideal', 'mental' control of events results in a short-circuiting of our genuine human powers.

It is the same preoccupation that explains Lawrence's attitude to science. This has provided much diversion to intellectuals of his time and after. Even the sympathetic Aldous Huxley finds it difficult to excuse a man who says he doesn't believe in evolution because he doesn't feel it in his solar plexus. Other critics have been more sarcastic still. Dr Tindall has a curious passage concerning *The Plumed Serpent*. He made the discovery that Lawrence got most of his information concerning Mexican history from an archaeologist, Zelia Nuttall, with whom he stayed. And Dr. Tindall comments: 'To express his gratitude Lawrence portrayed Mrs Nuttall . . . as the eccentric Mrs Norris. Depicting a host in such unflattering light might be considered a breach of decency on the part of another, but on the part of Lawrence it cannot be so construed, for she was a scientist and

[22] M. Buber, *Between Man and Man*, trans. R. Gregor Smith, Kegan Paul, 1947.

[23] R. Troisfontaines, *A La Rencontre de Gabriel Marcel*, La Sixaine, 1947, p. 30.

he could not abide a scientist.'[24] Now, quite apart from the injustice of this sarcasm—for in fact Mrs Norris is one of the few likeable Americans in the novel whom Kate 're-spected for her isolation and dauntlessness'—it is absurd to think that Lawrence rejected every kind of scientific discipline. He was suspicious of the merely academic scholar, but he was willing to make use of any ascertained results, and was certainly not, as Dr Tindall also suggests, taken in by amateur cranks (he sometimes *liked* cranks, of whom he knew only too many, but he soon saw through them). And even when Lawrence was critical of scientific dogmatism, he was often very shrewdly so.

> Pray, what is combustion? You can try and answer scientifically, till you are black in the face. All you can say is *that which happens* when matter is raised to a certain temperature —and so forth. . . . You might as well say, a word is that which happens when I open my mouth and squeeze my larynx and make various tricks with my throat muscles. All these explanations are so senseless. They describe the apparatus, and think they have described the event.[25]

It was a pity Lawrence had had no philosophical training. Considering the lack of it, he finds his way around remarkably well. But with it he would have found it easier to distinguish between mere subjectivism (which he frequently seems to present) and subjectivity, which is what his novels show to have been his genuine position. When his writing is at its best—and the style is the criterion for that—it is a demonstration *in concreto* that, in Martin Buber's words, 'all real life is meeting', whether a meeting of man with woman or a meeting of creature with creature.

> Know thyself means knowing at last that you *can't* know yourself. I can't know the Adam of red-earth which is me. . . . Neither can I know the serpent-listening Eve, which is the woman. . . . I have to take her at that. And we have to meet

[24] W. Y. Tindall, *D. H. Lawrence and Susan, his Cow*, p. 115.
[25] *Fantasia*, p. 141.

> as I meet a jaguar between the trees in the mountains, and advance and touch and risk it.[26]

That is one side. But this is not just irrationalism, as it is usually so facilely described.

> Let us accept our destiny. Man *can't* live by instinct, because he's got a mind. . . . Man has a mind, and ideas, so it is just puerile to sigh for innocence and naïve spontaneity . . . You've got to marry the pair of them [*sc.* emotions and the mind].[27]

And in spite of his own savage pilgrimage he was honest enough to see and admit that

> We can't go back. We can't go back to the savages: not a stride. We can be in sympathy with them. We can take a great curve in their direction, onwards. But we cannot turn the current of our life backwards, back to their soft warm twilight and uncreate mud.[28]

Is this mere inconsistency again? I think not. For though Lawrence did try to ' go back ', he was conscious all the time of what he was doing; and one must go back in order to discover that one cannot go back, and when one discovers that one also discovers what there is there to learn and what to avoid. And if we are insistent, and bludgeon Lawrence by saying that his dangerous talk about the importance of the ' blood ' was merely an open invitation to Rosenberg and the German Faith Movement to add ' and soil ', then we ought to pull ourselves up by remembering that it was mostly *our* fault. As Dr V. A. Demant, among other sociologists, has so often reminded us,[29] the Nazi (and other totalitarian) philosophy is the revenge taken upon modern society by the unconscious or preconscious elements which have been allowed to become dissociated from the intellectual levels at which we have tried to live.

26 *Assorted Articles,* p. 198.
27 *ibid.* ' On Human Destiny ', p. 215.
28 *Studies in Classical American Literature,* p. 138.
29 V. A. Demant, *The Religious Prospect, Christian Polity,* etc.

IV

'The Greeks, being sane, were pantheists and pluralists, and so am I.'[30] This is the nearest that Lawrence ever got to an actual formal label for his religious attachment. It is a curious statement, and not very accurate; but perhaps no one-word statement would be very accurate. There is no need to tell again the story of Lawrence's journey away from the Christian faith (if, indeed, he was ever there to journey away). The usual diet of Spencer, T. H. Huxley, J. M. Robertson, Haeckel and Co. had the usual effect; till he reached the stage, still in early life, of being able to write, 'There still remains a God, but not a personal God: a vast, shimmering impulse which waves onwards towards some end—I don't know what—taking no regard of the little individual, but taking regard for humanity.'[31] It is customary to talk about his early protestantism and the effect on him of his Methodist hymn-singing mother. It is important, however, to note a distinction here. First, Lawrence was brought up a Congregationalist, not a Methodist. Though he sometimes attended the meetings of the Primitive Methodists, and at moments admired a certain 'odd sense of wild mystery' about their singing,[32] he was generally rather scornful of them. Let me quote an autobiographical passage (1928) which is not, I fancy, very well known:

> I think it was good to be brought up a Protestant, and among Protestants a Nonconformist, and among Nonconformists, a Congregationalist. . . . I should have missed bitterly a direct knowledge of the Bible. . . . And in the Church of England one would hardly have escaped those snobbish hierarchies of class which spoil so much for a child. And the Primitive Methodists, when I was a boy, were always having 'revivals', and being 'saved', and I always had a horror of being saved. . . . The Congregationalists are the oldest Nonconformists, descendants of the Oliver Cromwell Independents.

[30] *Porcupine*, p. 135.
[31] Lawrence and Gelder, *Early Life of D. H. Lawrence*, p. 72.
[32] *Apocalypse*, p. 14.

They still had the Puritan tradition of no ritual. But they avoided the personal emotionalism which one found among the Methodists....

I am always glad we had the Bristol hymn-book, not Moody and Sankey. And I am glad our Scottish minister on the whole avoided sentimental messes such as 'Lead, Kindly Light', or even 'Abide With Me'. He had a healthy preference for healthy hymns (*e.g.*, 'At Even, ere the sun was set', or 'Fight the good fight').... The ghastly sentimentalism that came like leprosy over religion had not yet got hold of our colliery village.... Thirty-six years ago men, even Sunday School teachers, still believed in the fight for life and the fun of it. 'Hold the fort for I am coming'.... It was the battle-cry of a stout soul, and a fine thing too.[33]

But, secondly, it is important to remember that even the Independent variety of Nonconformity in which he was brought up bore only a distant relation to classical, orthodox Protestantism. Lawrence shows very little knowledge of the language of theological controversy—his account of the Reformation, in his little *Movements in European History,* is the usual liberal picture of emancipation. ('And so we see, step by step, great powers are broken down, and... individual men and women advance into freedom, freedom to believe as their soul prompts them, freedom to think as their mind sees well...' etc.).[34] I have come across only one passage where genuine theological concepts turn up, and that is, significantly perhaps, in a tussle between Ramón and his Roman Catholic Wife, Carlota, concerning the Quetzalcoatl religion, in *The Plumed Serpent:* 'All I want them to do', says Ramón, 'is to find the beginnings of the way to their own manhood, their own womanhood.... But these people don't assert any righteousness of their own,

[33] 'Hymns in a Man's Life,' *Evening News,* October 13, 1928, *Assorted Articles,* pp. 161 ff).
[34] *Movements,* cap. xii.

these Mexican people of ours. That makes me think that grace is still with them.'[35] And it is not surprising to find that in his chapter on 'The End of the Age of Faith' in the *History,* Lawrence gives a quite disproportionate place to the 'Introduction to the Everlasting Gospel' by Abbot Joachim of Flora, according to whom 'Judaism was the revelation of the Father: Christianity was the revelation of the Son: now men must prepare for the revelation of the Holy Ghost'.[36]

If Lawrence understood little of the genuine theological issues of Protestantism, still less did he understand of Catholicism. We may pardon incidental errors—such as Aaron's visit to Milan Cathedral between 4 and 5 p.m. to find Mass going on (which is hardly likely out of war-time).[37] But it goes, of course, deeper than that. There is in his early days an immediate revulsion against anything connected with Catholic worship or practice. Alvina, whose husband Cicio is of course a 'free thinker', goes into a Church in Casa Latina,

> and was almost sick with revulsion. The place was large, whitewashed, and crowded with figures in glass cases and *ex voto* offerings. The lousy-looking, dressed-up dolls, life-size and tinselly, that stood in the glass cases; the blood-streaked Jesus on the crucifix; the mouldering, mumbling filthy peasant women on their knees; all the sense of trashy, repulsive, degraded fetish-worship was too much for her....[38]

Yet pagan fetishes are all right—*e.g.,* for the Etruscans! It is significant that the only priest in the novels who is treated with sympathy is the Jesuit Monsignor who was the lover of 'The Lovely Lady', in the story of that name. (The jolly priest in ***The Boy in the Bush*** occurs in a passage

[35] *The Plumed Serpent,* p. 225.
[36] *Movements,* p. 173.
[37] *Aaron's Rod,* p. 194. Though Shakespeare's 'evening mass' at Verona is said to have had some historical basis (*Romeo and Juliet* IV. i. 38).
[38] *Lost Girl,* p. 364.

which is Miss Skinner's, to judge by the style.) Yet Lawrence had some quite good friends among the clergy—for instance, the padre at Oaxaca, according to Dorothy Brett.[39] And in his Introduction to Magnus' *Memoirs*[40] he describes how he goes to stay with Magnus in a Benedictine monastery south of Rome—Magnus is contemplating joining the order.

> It was very pleasant—not too sacred. One felt the monks were very human in their likes and their jealousies. It was rather like a group of dons in the dons' room at Cambridge, a cluster of professors in any college. . . .
>
> [But] I should die, if I had to stay up here. The past, the past, the beautiful and wonderful past, it seems to prey on my heart, I can't bear it.

And then he looks down at the plain below:

> That was another world. And how bitter, how barren a world! . . . And here above, sitting with the little stretch of pale, dry thistles around us, our back to a warm rock, we were in the Middle Ages. Both worlds were agony to me. But here, on the mountain top was worst: the past, the poignancy of the not-quite-dead past. 'I think one's got to go through with the life down there—get somewhere beyond it. One can't go back', I said to him [Magnus].

We remember that phrase, 'One can't go back', with its contradictions and associations, from another context.

But Lawrence's misunderstanding of Christianity goes deeper still. Mrs Carswell talks about 'The magnificently measured *Apocalypse*, with its profound understanding of Christianity, such an understanding as true repudiation requires.'[41] It is, as a matter of fact, from this very work that one could draw the most numerous instances of misunderstanding. For example, the misunderstanding of eschatology, in 'By the time of Christ all religion and all thought seemed to turn from the old worship and study of

[39] Dorothy Brett, *Lawrence and Brett*, p. 183.
[40] M. Magnus, *Memoirs of the Foreign Legion*, Introd., pp. 34, 42.
[41] C. Carswell, *Savage Pilgrimage*, p. 239.

vitality, potency, power, to the study of death and death-rewards, death-penalties and morals. All religion . . . became religion of postponed destiny . . .: eschatological, to use a pet word of the philosophers.'[42] Lawrence sees Christianity purely as 'love thy neighbour' or 'turn the other cheek'. We even find the extraordinary statement: '"Alone I did it!" is the proud assertion of the gentleman who attains Nirvana. And "Alone I did it!" says the Christian whose soul is saved.'[43] And he complains that the whole 'love-mode' is one-sided, inadequate: 'Love is not the only dynamic . . . it is only the one-half. There is always the other voluntary flow to reckon with, the intense motion of independence and singleness of self.'[44] An introduction to the ethics of St Thomas Aquinas, or even of Bishop Butler, would have told Lawrence how one-sided is his picture of Christian teaching about love. In his Introduction to an Edition of *The Grand Inquisitor,*[45] Lawrence expounds the Inquisitor's belief that 'Christianity is the ideal, but it is impossible. . . . Jesus *loved mankind for what it ought to be,* free and limitless. The Grand Inquisitor loves it for what it is, with all its limitations.' [Italics mine]. This phrase brings home to one the tragedy of Lawrence—that he was never introduced to anyone who could have given him an inkling of the ontological emphasis in authentic Christian and Catholic tradition. A few hours with, say, the Baron von Hügel (to mention only one of his contemporaries) might have opened unexpected doors to his exploration. Unfortunately there were few Christians who would have been personally sympathetic enough to effect a genuine meeting.

It will perhaps be said that fundamentally Lawrence's philosophy of life is utterly opposed to the Christian philosophy, since his is a philosophy of *Becoming.* Mr Richard

[42] *Apocalypse,* pp. 93, 130; *cf.* p. 101 *Sup.*
[43] *Phoenix,* p. 189.
[44] *Fantasia,* p. 117.
[45] *Phoenix,* p. 285 (1930).

Aldington, for instance, contrasts him with Joyce on this very score:[46] '*Ulysses* is static and solid, logically-planned, smelling of the lamp . . .', whereas Lawrence's work is so 'fluid, personal, imperfect', and therefore based on the concept of Becoming. It is true that usually Lawrence does proclaim the ultimacy of flux. 'Give me nothing fixed, set, static. . . . Give me the still, white seething, the incandescence and the coldness of the incarnate moment: the moment, the quick of all change and haste and opposition.'[47] But though he accepts the principle of relativity, he comes to see there must be some exceptions: 'Even relativity is only relative. Relative to the absolute. . . . The self is absolute. It may be relative to everything else in the universe. But to itself it is an absolute.'[48] It is part of Somers' contest with Kangaroo that the colonial folk are all surface and have no permanence about them; and it is Kangaroo, not Somers-Lawrence, who replies, 'I tell you, I *hate* permanency.' For Lawrence was looking for it. Though as novelist he is concerned with the flux of the Now and is therefore bound to lay most stress on Becoming, we must, he realizes, have Being in the background of our lives. 'Man is man, and woman is woman . . . as long as time lasts. In eternity, where infinite motion becomes rest, the two may be one. . . . In infinity, the spinning of the wheel upon the hub may be a frictionless whole, complete, an unbroken sleep that is infinite, motion that is utter rest.'[49]

And Lawrence states that the fundamental religious problem is, not whether God is, but what is our relation to Him. He has a very Kierkegaardian dialogue between two believers. (Merrild tells us, by the way, that he read and enjoyed Kierkegaard, though he does not say what work of his.)[50]

[46] Richard Aldington, Introduction to *Last Poems.*
[47] *Phoenix,* p. 219.
[48] *Kangaroo,* p. 314.
[49] *Phoenix,* p. 443.
[50] Knud Merrild, *A Poet and Two Painters,* p. 88.

I: Do you believe in God?
He: What the hell is that to you?
I: Oh, I'm just asking.
He: What about yourself?
I: Yes, I believe.
He: D'you say your prayers at night?
I: No. . . .
He: Then what use is your God to you?
I: He isn't the sort you pray to.
He: What do you do with him then?
I: It's what he does with me.
He: And what does he do with you?
I: Oh, I don't know. He uses me as the thin end of the wedge.

And his own comment is: ' I tell you, it isn't blasphemy. Ask any philosopher or theologian, and he'll tell you that the real problem for humanity isn't whether God exists or not. God always is, and we all know it. But the problem is, how to get at Him. The theologians try to find out: How shall man put himself into relation to God, into a living relation? Which is: How shall Man *find* God? That's the real problem.' [51]

V

And what sort of a God was it that Lawrence found? The nearest we can get is to say that He is the mighty, jealous God of the Old Testament—mixed up with other colours taken from Mithraism, Zoroastrianism, apocryphal Judaism, and other pagan religions, plus a generous, if highly eclectic, pinch of orthodox Christianity. Here Mr Eliot's comments are right. ' Lawrence had an awareness of something very important. He was aware that religion is not, and can never survive as, simply a code of morals. If (I think he would have said) you find you can only accept an " evil " religion, then for God's sake do, for that is far nearer the truth than not having any. . . . The religion which Lawrence would have liked to achieve is a religion of power and magic, of

[51] ' On Being Religious ', *Adelphi,* 1924: *Phoenix,* pp. 725-6.

control rather than propitiation.'[52] This is how Lawrence puts it. In church Will Brangwen

> did not want things to be intelligible. And he did not care about his trespasses, neither about the trespasses of his neighbour, when he was in church.... It was weekday stuff. ... In church, he wanted a dark, nameless emotion, the emotion of all the great mysteries of the passion.

And Ursula, as she grows, comes to think the same.

> Though she did not know it, her Sunday was very precious to her. She found herself in a strange, undefined place where her spirit could wander in dreams, unassailed.... There was Sin, the serpent, in whom was also wisdom.... But there was no *actual* Sin. If Ursula slapped Theresa across the face ... that was not Sin, the everlasting. It was misbehaviour.... Sin was absolute and everlasting; wickedness and badness were temporary and relative.

And it is at this stage that Lawrence begins to express his constant preoccupation with Resurrection, especially the Resurrection of the *Body*.

> The cycle of creation still wheeled in the Church year. After Christmas the ecstasy slowly sank and changed.... They moved quietly, a little wanness on the lips of the children, at Good Friday, feeling the shadow upon their hearts. Then, pale with a deathly scent, came the lilies of resurrection, that shone coldly till the Comforter was given.
>
> But why the memory of the wounds and the death? Surely Christ rose with healed hands and feet, sound and strong and glad? Surely the passage of the cross and the tomb was forgotten? But no—always the memory of the wounds, always the smell of the grave-clothes? A small thing was Resurrection, compared with the Cross and the death, in this cycle.[53]

It is highly significant, too, that Lawrence rejected totally the Eastern way. There were moments when he was per-

[52] T. S. Eliot, in *Revelation,* l.c. p. 34.
[53] *Rainbow,* p. 263.

suaded that India held out a hope for the world. His stay in Ceylon was, of course, very short; but he did do some studying, at second hand, of Hinduism and yoga, and had a long, close friendship with the Brewsters, the American Buddhists. But his reaction is clear:

> One realizes how very barbaric the substratum of Buddhism is. I shrewdly suspect that the high-flownness of Buddhism altogether exists mostly on paper: and that its denial of the soul makes it always rather barren, even if philosophically, etc., more perfect.[54]

Is he, perhaps, poking gentle fun at the Brewsters at the beginning of his tale, *Things?* An idealist couple from New England try ' " Indian thought "—meaning, alas, Mrs Besant '; but ' they simply hadn't enough *Seitzfleisch* to squat under a bho-tree and get to Nirvana by contemplating anything, least of all their own navels.'

Anyway, he wrote firmly to Brewster in 1926:

> What irritated me in you in the past was a way you had of looking on Buddhism as some sort of easy ether into which you could float away unresisted and unresisting.[55]

This rejection of the Eastern way left him free to consider the Christian way more sympathetically. And it is again the doctrine of the Resurrection of the Body that draws him most. Christians may find distasteful his story of *The Man Who Died.* And they may be shocked at his good-natured baptizing of an Indian student, Boshi Sen, in wine. (Lawrence asked him, 'Have you ever been baptized, Boshi?' ' No, but I shouldn't mind. The more gods we Hindus have, the better we like it.' Then Lawrence ceremoniously baptized him with wine, after which Boshi chanted a Sanskrit hymn.) [56] But there is no blasphemy where there is no belief.

[54] *Letters,* p. 542.
[55] *ibid.,* p. 652.
[56] E. and A. Brewster, *Reminiscences and Correspondence of D. H. Lawrence,* p. 292.

On the other hand, Lawrence himself was shocked at *hypocrisy*. When E. T. 's brother made an irreverent remark on returning from the chapel where he had just received Communion, Lawrence was quite angry.[57] It is significant that the Brewsters themselves noted a change in Lawrence in the last years of his life. Earlier he had remarked to a Brahmin, 'You don't really believe in God. You can't in this age. No, no, it is a conception mankind has exhausted: the word no longer has meaning.'[58] But in 1930 he said in a conversation with them, 'I intend to find God: I wish to realize my relation with Him. I do not any longer object to the word God. My attitude regarding this has changed. I must establish a conscious relation with God.'[59] And so we are ready for his statements on the Resurrection:

> The Churches, instead of preaching the Risen Lord, go on preaching the Christ-child and Christ Crucified. . . . I doubt whether the Protestant Churches will ever have the faith and the power of life to take the great step onwards, and preach Christ Risen. The Catholic Church might. In the countries of the Mediterranean, Easter has always been the greatest of holy days. . . . The Roman Catholic Church may still unfold this part of the Passion fully, and make men happy again. . . .[60]

We remember that in his *A Propos Lady Chatterley* he praised the Church for its defence of marriage and compared the Pope favourably with Mr Bernard Shaw's 'chief prostitute in Europe' on the subject of sex-knowledge. And he continued:

> The old Church knew best the enduring needs of man, beyond the spasmodic needs of today and yesterday. . . . For centuries the mass of people lived in this rhythm, under the Church. And it is down in the mass that the roots of

57 'E.T.', *A Memoir,* p. 86.
58 E. and A. Brewster, *Reminiscences and Correspondence of D. H. Lawrence,* p. 175.
59 *ibid.,* p. 224.
60 'The Risen Lord', *Everyman,* October 3, 1929 *(Assorted Articles,* pp. 110 ff).

> religion are eternal. When the mass of a people loses the religious rhythm, that people is dead, without hope. But Protestantism came and gave a great blow to the religious and ritualistic rhythm of the year, in human life. Nonconformity *almost* finished the deed. Now you have a poor, blind, disconnected people with nothing but politics and bank-holidays to satisfy the eternal human need of living in ritual adjustment to the cosmos in its revolutions. . . . Mankind has got to get back to the rhythm of the cosmos, and the permanence of marriage.[61]

And the last thing Lawrence ever wrote, a few days before he died, was the deeply sympathetic review of Eric Gill's *Art Nonsense and Other Essays:*[62]

> It seems to me there is more in [these] two paragraphs than in all Karl Marx or Professor Whitehead or a dozen other philosophers rolled together. . . .
>
> For belief, Mr Gill turns to the Catholic Church. Well, it is a great institution, and we all like to feel romantic about it. But the Catholic Church needs to be born again, quite as badly as the Protestant. I cannot feel there is much more belief in God in Naples or Barcelona, than there is in Liverpool or Leeds. . . . No, the Catholic Church has fallen into the same disaster as the Protestant: of preaching a *moral* God, instead of Almighty God, the God of strength and glory and might and wisdom: a ' good ' God, instead of a vital and magnificent God. . . . The Catholic Church in the cities is as dead as the Protestant Church. Only in the country, among peasants, where the old ritual of the season lives on in its beauty, is there still some living, instinctive ' faith ' in the God of Life.

The God of Life. That was what ultimately mattered to Lawrence. ' O Lord! ' he cries out to God in one place, ' how long will you submit to this Insurance Policy interpretation of the Universe? '—where God turns out to be ' a sort of superlative Mr Wanamaker, running the globe as a revolving drygoods store '.[63] When he hears of the suicide

[61] *A Propos of Lady Chatterley's Lover,* pp. 60, 79.
[62] *Book Collector's Quarterly,* October-December, 1933 (*Phoenix,* p. 396).
[63] *Phoenix,* p. 319.

of his American friend, the poet Harry Crosby, he remarks: 'That's all he could do with life, throw it away. How could he betray the great privilege of life?'[64] In Lawrence's one bad novel, *The Trespasser,* he does condone the suicide of Siegmund; but the fact that this is so obviously a crude device for solving difficulties in the plot precisely exhibits what a bad novel it is—Lawrence is not really *in* it at all. So God is the God of life, and man is free, he is not a behaviourist, he must act 'with the blood', but it will be he who is acting.

And it is this, finally, which 'explains' Lawrence himself. For we must insist again that he is to be judged, not as priest, prophet or even medicine-man, but as a writer. If his works do not show the living tissue of which his theorizings and exhortations are only the tabular analysis, then the theories are not worth the breath they took to utter. The final proof that they do show this living tissue is given, I believe, by the discovery after his death of a little sheaf of poems, afterwards published as *Last Poems.*[65] After the cheap, clever, but often tawdry *Pansies,* the appearance of these last poems is something of a new birth itself. Indeed, they were a resurrection from one of Lawrence's many deaths—his penultimate bout of sickness. And the very movement of the verse is a rising to life again.

> Now it is autumn and the falling fruit
> and the long journey towards oblivion.
>
> Have you built your ship of death, O have you?
> O build your ship of death, for you will need it.
>
> And can a man his own quietus make
> with a bare bodkin?
> Surely not so! for how could murder, even self-murder
> ever a quietus make?

[64] E. and A. Brewster, *Reminiscences and Correspondence of D. H. Lawrence,* p. 308.
[65] Edited by Richard Aldington, Heinemann, 1935.

O let us talk of quiet that we know,
that we can know, the deep and lovely quiet
of a strong heart at peace!

Now launch the small ship, now as the body dies
and life departs, launch out, the fragile soul . . .
And everything is gone, the body is gone
completely under, gone, entirely gone.
The upper darkness is heavy as the lower,
between them the little ship
is gone
It is the end, it is oblivion.

So far it is all a fall away, down, down to extinction. And if we were to leave it there, it would be justifiable to say, as for instance Mr Norman Nicholson does, that 'the oblivion is of death. . . . This is the end to which Lawrence's denial of the intellect has brought him, to the negation of all consciousness, to the negation of all life, to death. His genius draws him to the logical conclusion of this thought, to the death-will.'[66] But it is not fair to stop there. Before the end of the poem there is a section which lifts up, and explains why the Ship is worth building, why the journey is worth undertaking.

And yet out of eternity a thread
separates itself on the blackness
a horizontal thread
that fumes a little with pallor upon the dark.

Wait, wait! even so, a flush of yellow
and strangely, O chilled wan soul, a flush of rose.

The flood subsides, and the body, like a worn sea-shell
emerges strange and lovely. . . .

And so Lawrence recurs to his favourite symbol, in the poem *Phoenix:*

Are you willing to be sponged out, erased, cancelled,
made nothing?

If not, you will never really change.

[66] N. Nicholson, *Man and Literature,* SCM Press, 1944, p. 82.

The phoenix renews her youth
only when she is burnt, burnt alive, burnt down
to hot and flocculent ash.
Then the small stirring of a new small bud in the nest
with strands of down like floating ash
shows that she is renewing her youth like the eagle
Immortal bird

and

So let me live that I may die
Eagerly passing over from the entanglement of life
to the adventure of death, in eagerness
turning to death as I turn to beauty
to the breath, that is, of new beauty unfolding in death.

CHAPTER SIX

RETROSPECT

I

THE sieve of twenty years * and a second world-war has been shaken violently from side to side. We must now ask what of Lawrence comes through it. The question is put as well as could be by Mr John Lehmann in a lecture on 'The Search for the Myth',[1] addressed to the Greeks in the autumn of 1946:

> Lawrence means surprising little today to the young intellectuals of my country. A Lawrence enthusiast would say, perhaps, that it is simply because his books have been all but unobtainable for so long, and a revival will come when they are printed again. Lawrence is indeed, at his best, an amazing artist, and for that he will again be given due honour in the course of time; but I cannot help feeling that his present eclipse has other reasons. We have fought the Satanism of Hitler for seven years; we have come to recognize that the precious ore in the values that our Christian heritage has brought with it is more important than the dross. Can the myth which we are looking for be a denial of the world of love? Should it not rather be a new exploration of that world? It is not new creeds, the worship of a barbarous plumed serpent, that we crave: but the restatement of some of the most ancient truths of our civilization within the conditions of our modern life.

The first defence of Lawrence has already been conceded here: that if he was a great artist then he will be permanently valid whatever the changes of fashion. It is good, in view of his neglect, that this should be conceded. And yet,

* This was written in 1950.

[1] John Lehmann, in *Penguin New Writing,* no. 30, 1947.

to acclaim him as 'artist' and then to dismiss what he had to say, is to make just the separation of 'art' from 'message' which it has been the main theme of this book to refuse.

It may appear a paradox, but I should claim that one of the great virtues of Lawrence was his sense of the ISness rather than the OUGHTness of religion. Indeed, we have seen (p. 133, *above*) that his quarrel with Christianity was that, as he thought—wrongly, we believe—Christianity had not that sense. This is precisely an emphasis that is needed at a time when, in some desperation, so many are turning to, or trying to discover, a saving myth. For there is a danger that such a myth, adopted as a physic or a salve, will become either a mere lyric aspiration or else a moralism. I am not going to defend Lawrence's snake-dancers or Etruscan ancestor-worship. But it is important to see that he believed in his dark gods not because they 'worked', but because they were true. And so, man's destiny is the bringing into full being of that which already is:

> The final aim of every living thing, creature, or being is the full achievement of itself. . . . [So] the day is richer for a poppy, the flame of another phoenix is filled in to the universe, something is which was not. . . . And I wish it were true of us. I wish we were all like kindled bonfires on the edge of space, marking out advance-posts.[2]

This is the context in which to appreciate Lawrence's stress upon the subconscious levels of existence. Nor do I think that we can yet afford to neglect this. Lawrence would say, I suppose, that our deepest problems arise here, and therefore that to adopt some myth, consciously and deliberately, because others have failed us, is still to leave the profoundest scars unhealed. I should naturally agree with Mr Lehmann that we need a new exploration of the 'world of love'; but not as dictating an imperative. Our loss of this world of love is not, at its deepest, due to a deliberate and conscious repudiation of it, but to a fissure of *being*. The

[2] *Study of Hardy* (*Phoenix*, p. 403).

totalitarian deliberate rejection of love is not a sudden 'sport' in man's moral evolution: it has itself to be accounted for, and its explanation is that man today has his roots, alas, in a dwindling subsoil. And in the classical Christian tradition love is the very constitution of creation as it comes from the hand of God: to deny it is to act *contra naturam*. Therefore, if 'de-naturing' has happened to some extent at the pre-conscious level, through the sundering of intellect from instinct, then we cannot be 're-natured' merely by consciously wishing ourselves back into a world of love. We have hinted that Lawrence's greatest weakness is his un-acquaintance with this classical Christian tradition. But I think that unawares he was saying more than he knew when he spoke of the real fantasia as happening in the unconscious. Another contemporary critic of great sensitiveness has, in an otherwise admirable book, made the same criticism of Lawrence as Mr Lehmann.[3] 'The two modern writers who have described the natural man most penetratingly and eloquently, D. H. Lawrence and Henri de Montherlant'—an odd combination!— 'are therefore almost of necessity Fascists by implication.' But Lawrence at his best does not, I believe, really describe, or even mean to describe 'natural man' *tout court;* he is dimly aware that what Christians would call 'super-nature' and he would call 'the gods' is necessary to make, or re-make, the de-natured into the natural. If the Christian 'myth', as a real operative element in our collective culture, is dead, it is Lawrence who felt this most deeply and agonizingly: and it is he, too, who has seen most clearly that if it is ever to be recovered it will be, not by programmes or research, still less by moral exhortation, but by resurrection.

It was a very un-Lawrentian philosopher, the late R. G. Collingwood, who said that in a world saturated with

[3] Edwin Muir, 'The Natural Man and the Political Man' in *Essays on Literature and Society,* Hogarth, 1949. This essay is reprinted from *New Writing and Daylight,* Summer, 1942.

amusement-art, 'the more magic we produce the better'.[4] It does not seem that since Lawrence's death we have learned any better the lesson what happens when the gods are deceased. And it is significant that where there have been, in this intervening period, real signs of a re-awakening—as in the art of Mr Henry Moore—it has been precisely at the point where what we might call a primitive pan-sacramentalism has been at work. We are not yet perhaps in a position to be too fastidious about the pantheon: let us recover the gods before we start rationing them.

The real gravamen against Lawrence will (for the Christian, at any rate) lie in the fundamental inconsistency from which his thought so often suffers. The 'pantheist' elements in his writings cannot really be made to square with the 'transcendent' elements in his conception of the 'mighty', 'living God'. This is a permanent problem for pantheism. A writer with whom Lawrence would have had many sympathies, M. Gustave Thibon, has put it profoundly: 'It is precisely pantheism which most betrays the divinity of things. It begins by sacrificing the transcendent Being to its levelling kind of monism, by diluting God into the world. After that, how can it rediscover the authentic divine imprint in things? . . . The negation of the creator deflowers the creation: it is no longer possible to divinize the world after one has "cosmified" God.'[5]

II

But Lawrence saves himself by eschewing consistent pantheism. And we can see this more clearly when he is being the 'artist' than when he is analysing or talking his 'polyanalytics'. Even hostile critics are agreed that Lawrence's supreme achievement was to find expression for

[4] R. G. Collingwood, *The Principles of Art* OUP, 1938, p. 276.
[5] G. Thibon, *Destin de L'Homme,* Desclée de Brouwer, 1943, p. 23.

states of being hitherto almost unexplored, or at any rate unexpressed. It is in the relatedness of the self with the other-self, and of the self with the sub-self—trees, horses, snakes, rocks, seed and flower—that the human unconscious can meet the conscious mind and so the self become aware of the self. And when this happens, the gods are pricking nature into life. As one reads Lawrence's descriptions one is suddenly aware that he is not merely describing: he is pushing an electric current through the bit of the world that stands before him, and immediately that world falls apart into two—one half of it suddenly becomes erect, shudders and bristles with life; the other half burns in a flash and shrivels into dead grey ash. Does not one feel this in the very structure of his language?

> He drank enough
> And lifted his head, dreamily, as one who has drunken,
> And flickered his tongue like a forked night on the air,
>   so black,
> Seeming to lick his lips,
> And looked around like a god, unseeing, into the air,
> And slowly turned his head,
> And slowly, very slowly, as if thrice adream,
> Proceeded to draw his slow length curving round
> And climb again the broken bank of my wall-face.

There is the voice and the rhythm of life, the alternate hard consonantal sounds giving us the 'quick' of existence, balanced by the smooth drawling vowels for the deliberate and controlled sense of perfect command. And then, by contrast, comes the voice of so-called civilization:

> I looked round, I put down my pitcher,
> I picked up a clumsy log
> And threw it at the water-trough with a clatter...
> And immediately I regretted it.
> I thought how paltry, how vulgar, what a mean act!
> I despised myself and the voices of my accursed human
>   education.
>
> *(Snake)*

This is the dead prose (clicking, like false teeth) of unsympathy and unawareness. Even Lawrence's simplest observations of 'nature'—the

> Swallows with spools of dark thread sewing the shadows together
>
> *(Bat)*

or this brilliant painting of *Turkey-Cock*

> Your wattles are the colour of steel-slag which has been red hot
> And is going cold,
> Cooling to a powdery, pale-oxydized sky-blue

have a depth behind or beneath them which makes them more than mere 'nature poetry'. Perhaps the most powerful instance is the description of the bull, in *St Luke*

> A wall, a bastion,
> A living forehead with its slow whorl of hair
> And a bull's large, sombre, glancing eye
> And glistening, adhesive muzzle
> With cavernous nostrils where the wind runs hot
> Snorting defiance
> Or greedily snuffling behind the cows.

Before ever we come to the explicit reference, later in the poem, to the bull's 'daimon' we are aware of something more than just one particular animal standing there. Even in Lawrence's earlier, more lyrical poems there is a suspicion of something deeper; as, for instance, in the lovely *History*

> And then in a strange, grey hour
> We lay mouth to mouth, with your face
> Under mine like a star on the lake,
> And I covered the earth and all space.
> The silent, drifting hours
> Of morn after morn
> And night drifting up to the night
> Yet no pathway worn. . . .

Still more, in 'Craving for Spring':

Oh, yes, the gush of spring is strong enough
to toss the globe of the earth like a ball on a water-jet
dancing sportfully;
as you see a tiny celluloid ball tossing on a squirt of water
for men to shoot at, penny-a-time, in a booth at a fair.

Their achievement is to convey to us the sense that what is shown as alive owes its aliveness to something behind or above—to the transcendent.

To state the same thing in another way: Lawrence was an astonishing diagnostician of life. His sensitive nose could smell death a mile away, long before the physician could discern the slightest organic signs of decay. Here it is, observed in an old chapel deacon:

> The father sat big and unheeding in his chair, his eyes vacant, his physique wrecked. He let them do as they would, he fell to pieces. And yet some power, involuntary, like a curse, remained in him. The very ruin of him was like a lodestone that held them in its control. The wreck of him still dominated the house, in his dissolution even he compelled their being. (*The Christening*)

Or, in terrible contrast with a false attempt at life in an unreal marriage, this (the wife is washing the body of her husband, brought in dead from the pit):

> The man's mouth was fallen back, slightly open under the cover of the moustache. The eyes, half shut, did not show glazed in the obscurity. Life with its smoky burning gone from him, had left him apart and utterly alien to her. . . . In her womb was ice of fear, because of this separate stranger with whom she had been living as one flesh. . . . And her soul died in her for fear: she knew she had never seen him, he had never seen her, they had met in the dark. . . .
> (*Odour of Chrysanthemums*)

Or again, in a very different context, there is this uncovering of a death in life [of Owen, the American]:

> So empty, and waiting for circumstances to fill him up. Swept with an American despair of having lived in vain, or

> of not having *really* lived. Having missed something. Which fearful misgiving would make him rush like mechanical steel filings to a magnet, towards any crowd in the street. And then all his poetry and philosophy gone with the cigarette-end he threw away, he would stand craning his neck in one more frantic effort to *see*—just to *see*. . . . And then, after he'd seen an old ragged woman run over by a motor-car and bleeding on the floor, he'd come back to Kate pale at the gills, sick, bewildered, daunted, and yes, yes, glad he'd seen it. It was Life! (*The Plumed Serpent*)

And finally, in a story which Lawrence once described as his own favourite, there is a remarkable passage in which he contrasts the sterile triviality of life in a localized time with the terrible but vivid existence of eternity, peopled with the years:

> When, in the city, you wear your white spats and dodge the traffic with the fear of death down your spine, then you are safe from the terrors of infinite time. The moment is your little islet in time, it is the spatial universe that careers round you.
>
> But once isolate yourself on a little island in the sea of space, and the moment begins to heave and expand in great circles, the solid earth is gone, and your slippery, naked dark soul finds herself out in the timeless world, where the chariots of the so-called dead dash down the old streets of centuries, and souls crowd on the foot-ways that we, in the moment, call bygone years. The souls of all the dead are alive again, and pulsating actively around you.
>
> (*The Man Who Loved Islands*)

We have seen, especially in chapter three, how Lawrence could sense the death of a country or a civilization; and he so conveys that sense to us that we can never look quite the same way again at the places and societies he describes for us. This is the context in which to assess Lawrence the ' agrarian '. He was never merely cranky about ' back-to-the-landism', and his correspondence with Mr Rolf Gardiner shows how cautious he was in committing himself to it. There are those who have complained that—largely owing to his health—he never really experienced work on the land, and that this weakens his advocacy of it. But Lawrence did work as a farm labourer in Cornwall during his exile there in the 1914–18 war, and by all accounts worked very hard; and his friends in Mexico all testify to his practical efficiency in the house or in the fields. As writer, his attacks on industrialism and his pleas for a return to 'nature' arose out of his sense of the kinship of being, his intuitive knowledge of hierarchies profounder than the visible. And his protests against the 'One-World' view (*v. sup.*, p. 73). derive from the same, fundamentally religious, sense; his awareness of the 'spirit of place' links him with those regional writers who are likely, it seems, to become more, not less, prominent as our technical energies are expended on 'global' enterprises. The lecture by Mr Lehmann from which this chapter started contains one quotation which is directly relevant here. Mr Lehmann cites the Greek poet, Capetanakis, discussing the Greek painter, Ghika:

> Ghika's symbols no longer have the general abstract character which they had till now. They are closely linked with the soil and sky of a definite place. But it is just for that reason that their artistic significance has increased. The more precise the language of art becomes the wider becomes its meaning and the deeper.

Mr Lehmann does not refer to Lawrence at this point; but Lawrence would certainly have applauded the quotation. The sense of the local, true and vital in its very locality, is part of the deep appreciation of the particular which is the central quality in art, and Lawrence expresses this himself. 'One must be limited', muses Kate in *The Plumed Serpent* (p. 470). 'If one tries to be unlimited, one becomes horrible.'

It is thus, too, that we can understand and still value Lawrence's battle with 'scientism'. At a time when Wells was still in the ascendant, Lawrence must have seemed mad, not merely to have challenged that ascendancy, but to have challenged it with such flimsy, imprecise, poetical weapons; surely 'the belly' has a poor chance against the well-organized armoury of rationalist science? Yet of course

Lawrence was digging deeper than the level at which the romantic attack upon science was so often conducted. Discussing Russian civilization once, he observed:

> The whole accumulation of western ideas, ideals and inventions was poured in a mass into their hot and undeveloped consciousness, and worked like wild yeast. It produced a century of literature, from Pushkin to Rozanov, and then the wild working of this foreign leaven had ruined, for the time being, the very constitution of the Russian people. . . . Too sudden civilization always kills. It kills the South Sea Islanders: it killed the Russians, more slowly and perhaps more effectively.[6]

'Too sudden civilization always kills'—that is the point. And Lawrence's battle with the mechano-mathematical mentality of the West was not a denial of science or of civilization, but an attempt to point the way to a better kind of science. And this links Lawrence with the thinkers known as 'existentialists', with some of whom, as we shall see, he has certain striking affinities. After all, he wrote a preface to an English translation (again, as in the case of Rozanov, by his friend Kotelianski) of a work by one of the recognized precursors of 'existentialism'—Leo Chestov.[7] And Chestov had there made remarks like:

> The habit of logical thinking kills imagination. . . . The nearer we approach the ultimate questions of existence, in our departure from logicality, the more deadly [*sc.* we suppose] becomes the state of error we fall into [*sc.* but we are wrong].
>
> The only way to guard against positivism . . . is to cease to fear any absurdities, whether rational or metaphysical, and systematically to reject all the services of reason.
>
> No theory can survive man's reluctance to believe in it.

[6] Review of Rozanov, *Fallen Leaves* (*Phoenix*, p. 390).

[7] Introduction to Leo Chestov, *All Things are Possible,* trans. Kotelianski, Secker, 1920. Lawrence, by the way, seems to have influenced the translation at points, as we saw he did in the case of Rozanov. Kotelianski makes Chestov at one point use the unlikely, but Lawrentian, expletive 'Basta' (p. 181).

> Kant, and after him Schopenhauer, was exceeding fond of the epithet ' disinterested '. . . . Had he chanced to be brought amongst Russian peasants he would have had to change his opinion. . . . There the highest activity is interested activity.

This last quotation is very revelant. Since Chestov's, and Lawrence's, day we have learned better that the instrument cannot be altogether isolated from the intellect that uses it; that Intention is the starting-point, indeed, of the quest for Truth; that what we find depends enormously upon what we are looking for. There is, we see, no such thing as pure intellection or pure scientific analysis abstracted from all purpose. And Lawrence, in his undisciplined, but quick, intuitive way, was aware of it.

III

Supreme in the ' nature ' Lawrence investigates is, however, the place of encounter between human persons. Here in a few lines of nervous, vivid prose Lawrence can show us, on one side a dead relationship, on the other a living. What an astonishing amount is achieved in a few words like this—speaking of Ethel Cane, who would never let men go far with her—

> She had a terrible way of saying ' I'm having none of that! ' —like hitting a mirror with a hammer.
>
> (*None of That*)

Or, describing poor Henry Lubbock, who lived for a time with Virginia Bodmin, but never plucked up courage to marry her, because he found that living with her was really living with her mother:

> So he backed out. He didn't jump out, or bolt, or carve his way out at the sword's point. He sort of faded out, distributing his departure over a year or more.
>
> (*Mother and Daughter*)

These are both dead relationships; for the living—well, there is the vast field of his novels and stories to help oneself from. For a brief example, what about this? (Hilda, now in love with Arthur Pilbeam, a gamekeeper, meets her old lover, Syson; she talks to him about Arthur, and admits that he comes short in some ways, compared with him, Syson.)

> 'The stars aren't the same with him,' she said. '*You* could make them flash and quiver, and the forget-me-nots come up at me like phosphorescence. . . .'
>
> (*The Shades of Spring*)

(A good account, by the way, of what Lawrence does for us with his prose.)

It is interesting to compare Lawrence's account of these relationships with that of the 'existentialists'. One critic has said of these latter that it is precisely '*le thême de l'autre*' that is their great contribution to philosophy.[8] Classical philosophy, this critic avers, strangely neglected this study: '. . . Knowledge, the outside world, myself, the soul and the body, the mind, God, and the future life—the problem created by association with other people never assumes in Classical philosophy the same importance as the other problems. At one stroke, Existentialism has raised it to its central position. . . .' The attention of sociology and collectivism 'was concentrated upon social organization and not upon the nature of the connexion between one man's existence and the next man's . . . the existentialist critique has a direct bearing on the danger of the factor of estrangement, which lies in wait for every existent who conducts his relations with men solely on the plan-of-organization basis.' We need not enter into a detailed discussion of the various analyses given by different, and competing, existentialists of this problem of inter-subjective relations. The point is that Lawrence to a remarkable degree understood the problem himself. And in the end his answers would, I think, certainly

[8] Emmanuel Mounier, *Existentialist Philosophies—an Introduction*, Rockliff, 1948.

be nearer those given by the Christian than by the atheist branch of existentialism. It is true that he is very much aware of the danger of 'alienation'; he is no less clear than M. Jean-Paul Sartre, that even love may become a mode of domination. M. Sartre describes this as an attempt to possess the other's liberty over me by entering into his subjectivity: which may then become an offering of myself as object to the other; as a result of which I (subject) having failed to reach the other—for I have only given him myself (object) —may then try to have my revenge by treating myself violently as object. Hence masochism.[9] All this analysis, in less technical terms of course, seems to me to have been remarkably foreshadowed in some of the lucubrations of Lilly (*Aaron's Rod*) and of Somers (*Kangaroo*). But at the same time it is certain that Lawrence would not have remained satisfied with what seems so often to be the metaphysically solipsistic conclusions of M. Sartre. (True, Sartre rejects the accusation; but his defence still leaves us with what can only be described, illogically no doubt, as a 'pluralistic solipsism'.) Lawrence would agree that the kind of love analysed above is, as a solution of the inter-subjective problem, 'unauthentic' (to use Heidegger's phrase). But he would go on to claim that there *is* an authentic sort. Above all, in his treatment of sexuality. According to Sartre, the sexual approach is still in the end an attempt at reducing the other's freedom, by stripping him to his bare flesh: and then, he says, all I possess of the other is 'leavings' (*une dépouille*), and not the other as subject; this indicates to me that he is inaccessible, and so I easily become a sadist to revenge myself for the unattainable.[10] (It does not seem to have been observed, by the way, by writers on Sartre, that in his treatment of sexual relations in *L'Etre et le Néant,* it is nowhere made clear whether Sartre is talking of hetero- or of homosexual relations. That his actual analysis would apply indifferently to either is a highly significant indication

[9] J. P. Sartre, *L'Etre et le Néant,* part iii, cap. 3.
[10] *ibid.,* pp. 431-84.

of its limitations.) Sartre's own disciple, Mme. Simone de Beauvoir, has criticized Lawrence's 'myth' of sex.[11] She says (not without some justice) that his novels are above all concerned with the 'education of women'; that except for Paul Morel in *Sons and Lovers* the heroes do not progress—they know all the secrets of wisdom from the start; and that what the women have to learn to do is simply to submit to the male. (This last accusation is not altogether true; in many of the novels—and short stories especially—this female submission itself constitutes the tragic theme.) But it is not obvious that the authoress of *The Blood of Others* can provide a fuller and more satisfactory alternative. Anyway, it is certain that Lawrence would never consent that the body (flesh) is but *une dépouille* of the self, or that it is the final barrier to intersubjective communication. On the contrary, it is for him a central point of man's connectedness. And the Christian doctrine of creation would imply the same.

There is, in fact, another school of existentialist writers—the Christian or near-Christian, Marcel, Berdyaev, Buber, Jaspers—who believe that communion *is* possible. And however much at times Lawrence seems to be exalting sex over every other element in creation, he always at bottom sees it as something within a larger whole.

> No man ever had a wife unless he served a great predominant purpose. Otherwise, he has a lover, a mistress. No matter how much she may be married to him, unless his days have a living purpose, constructive or destructive, but a purpose beyond her and all she stands for; unless his days have this purpose, and his soul is really committed to his purpose, she will not be a wife, she will be only a mistress and he will be her lover.[12]

Here is the Christian-existentialist theme of 'engagement'. And Lawrence is at his greatest when he expresses it—as indeed, existentialism requires—not in conceptual terms, but

[11] *The Second Sex*, Cape, 1953.
[12] *Fantasia*, p. 175.

in his writing, his poems and his novels. There is *his* engagement, requiring generosity, requiring the devotion he gave it through all the years of opposition and disappointment and misunderstanding:

> Give, and it shall be given unto you
> is still the truth about life.
> But giving life is not so easy.
> It doesn't mean handing it out to some mean fool, or letting the living dead eat you up.
> It means kindling the life-quality where it was not,
> even if it's only in the whiteness of a washed pocket-handkerchief.[13]

And is there any guarantee that this 'engagement' is worthwhile, that there is a greater purpose within which our lesser dedications may find their meaning? Here is Lawrence's answer to that—his final denial of pessimism:

> It is not easy to fall out of the hands of the living God.
> They are so large, and they cradle so much of a man.
> It is a long time before a man can get himself away.
> Even through the greatest blasphemies, the hands of the living God still continue to cradle him.[14]

[13] 'We Are Transmitters' (from *Collected Poems*).
[14] 'Abysmal Immortality' *(ibid.)*.

INDEX